THE MEXICAN WAR

The

THE CHICAGO HISTORY OF AMERICAN CIVILIZATION

Daniel J. Boorstin, EDITOR

Mexican War

By Otis A. Singletary

 THE UNIVERSITY OF CHICAGO PRESS

CHICAGO AND LONDON

This book is also available in a clothbound edition from
THE UNIVERSITY OF CHICAGO PRESS

THE UNIVERSITY OF CHICAGO PRESS, CHICAGO & LONDON
The University of Toronto Press, Toronto 5, Canada

© *1960 by The University of Chicago. Published 1960*
Fourth Impression 1965
Printed in the United States of America

For

GLORIA

Editor's Preface

The Mexican War was a melodrama of the irritations and internal conflicts that have continued to plague American democracy at war. For the clarity with which it illustrates these conflicts it has no equal. Also, no passage in our history better illustrates the price in military effectiveness that we have had to pay for our tradition of civilian command and for our regular periodic system of national elections. Mr. Singletary shows how the conduct of generals on the battlefield was affected by political ambition. Then, as now, the road ran direct from the field of military glory to the White House.

Too often the Mexican War has been passed over as a kind of prologue to the Civil War. In the textbooks it always seems to crop up as an early episode in the career of a Lincoln, a Lee, a Grant, or a Beauregard, who were destined to go on to greater things.

As Mr. Singletary shows us, we have a number of reasons for wanting to forget this war. It was an offensive war. Undertaken as a political decision by people ignorant of the military problems, the Mexican War resembled most of our later military enterprises. The same exigencies of federal representative government which had drawn us into the conflict also prevented us from considering calmly the implications of our entry, from weighing the cost of war or the benefits of victory. The very fact that the war was limited to one small part of this hemisphere, that it was conducted without allies, and that it was relatively unconfused by world issues, makes it a particularly vivid illustration of our domestic shortcomings.

An American Tolstoy could hardly have done better than invent the story of the Mexican War and fill it with the very same characters—great and small—who move across Mr. Singletary's pages. The tragedy of frustrated ambition, of ignorant men forced to pretend to knowledge, of weak men forced to seem decisive, of men forced by circumstances to struggle against each other instead of against their common enemy—all these appear as vividly on the deserts and in the hills of Mexico and on the Texas border as they do on the march to Moscow or in the grand arena of Waterloo. In war, as in politics, it is the small things that make the difference. And Mr. Singletary has been remarkably successful (despite the brevity of his book) in showing us the constant importance of coincidence, of personality, and of human pettiness in affecting the outcome.

By putting the Mexican War in the main stream of our history, Mr. Singletary makes an important addition to the "Chicago History of American Civilization," which aims to make each aspect of our culture a window to all our history. The series contains two kinds of books: a *chronological* group, which provides a coherent narrative of American history from its beginning to the present day, and a *topical* group, which deals with the history of varied and significant aspects of Amer-

Editor's Preface

ican life. This book is one of the topical group. Twenty-odd titles in the series are in preparation. A number of other volumes are projected which will eventually deal with all the major wars in which we have had a part.

Daniel J. Boorstin

Table of Contents

Illustrations

MAPS

PLATES

Prologue

In May, 1846, the American people found themselves involved in what was to become the first successful offensive war in their history. Although American armies, in the two years that followed, won spectacular victories in the field, there were other consequences of the war with Mexico far transcending in importance purely military ones. It ended with finality a long, drawn-out boundary dispute, incorporated vast new territories into the national domain, brought into the Union new peoples to be assimilated, and raised new problems that would have to be solved. It focused our attention on the Pacific and sharpened our interest in the Far East. It made possible the Gold Rush of '49 and made necessary the Compromise of '50. What may appear to have been just another military exercise was instead a profoundly significant event, one that altered the face of the nation and helped shape its future course.

From a strictly military point of view, the war was a smashing success. In eighteen hectic months of combat, United States forces won an unbroken string of victories in northern Mexico, occupied the enemy provinces of New Mexico and California, landed on the beach below Veracruz, and fought their way inland to occupy for the first time an enemy capital.

On the broad canvas of nineteenth-century military affairs, the war was yet another illustration of the comparative ineffectiveness of the European military system when employed in the New World. European influence on the Mexican army was plainly apparent and its effects were in many ways detrimental. It was an army woefully short on morale, one in which a wide gulf separated the troops, enlisted from the lower classes, from their officers, who, because they had obtained their commissions through family or political connections, were frequently ignorant of the military profession. It was an army that preferred to fight at long range with artillery and musket, that had little enthusiasm for close work with the bayonet. It was an army that was frequently poorly led. Even Santa Anna, by all odds the ablest Mexican general in the war, lacked the decisiveness that marks the great commander. It was an army that made serious miscalculations, pinning its hopes on the cavalry only to see them smashed by the devastatingly effective light, mobile, "flying" artillery and by the deadly accuracy of American riflemen. In markmanship, American soldiers were surpassed by none. They were, in the main, men who had long been accustomed to hunt for their own food and who had, in the process, become experts through necessity. The troops that fought under Taylor at Buena Vista, largely recruited from frontier states, were the same breed that had stood with Jackson and had slaughtered "Britain's finest" in the swamps outside New Orleans in early 1815. In its own way, then, the Mexican War was but another variation of an old theme; it was, with purely local modifications, the story of Braddock and Burgoyne and Pakenham all over again.

In the narrower framework of American military history, the war with Mexico has special significance because of the number of "firsts" associated with it. It was not only our first successful offensive war and our first successful occupation of an enemy capital, it was also the first of our wars in which a significant number of West Pointers played an important role. The Military Academy paid its first real dividend to the American people in the mid-forties, when both Scott and Taylor were able to surround themselves with capable, competent, well-trained junior officers. It was the first war in our history in which martial law was declared on foreign soil; by General Order 20, promulgated on February 19, 1847, at Tampico, Scott authorized the establishment of military commissions to try offenses committed by and against his men while they were operating beyond the territorial limits of the United States. It was, furthermore, the first in which the modern war correspondent made his appearance; men like George Wilkins Kendall of the New Orleans *Picayune* went in person to the theater of operations, traveled with the troops as they fought their way into Mexico and relayed their firsthand observations of the war back to their newspapers with such dispatch that their readers not infrequently learned of any important occurrence at the front before the Secretary of War did. It was this war that provided the first significant combat experience for that group of young men who were soon to make larger reputations in another war. Both Lee and Grant learned there lessons they would one day apply on battlefields far removed from Mexico, and the roster of officers who served below the Rio Grande—including such names as Jackson, Longstreet,

Beauregard, the two Johnstons, Sherman, McClellan, and Hooker, to mention but a few—sounds like a roll call of Civil War commanders.

Yet, strangely enough, the Mexican War, in spite of its national and international significance, has never really caught the fancy of the American reading public. There are no Mexican War Round Tables, no Mexican War Book Clubs and few persons outside the historical profession have ever heard of Doniphan's Expedition or could identify, with anything approaching accuracy, Mr. Nicholas Trist. Even Winfield Scott, the able soldier who engineered the conquest of Mexico City, when he is remembered at all, is remembered rather vaguely as a bumbling old incompetent in the advanced stages of senility who got in the way of important people during the early days of the Civil War.

The relative obscurity of the Mexican War is attributable to a number of circumstances. In the first place, it was not one of those massive affairs we have come to know by the name of "total war." It was in many ways a limited or restricted war; limited in the numbers engaged as well as in the numbers affected by it. It was not war of whole populations, by whole populations, against whole populations, nor was it accompanied by total destruction. In fact it was not even a total victory, since it was officially terminated by a negotiated rather than a dictated peace. Then, too, the Mexican War has been neglected for the simple reason that it has, historically speaking, been forced to live in the shadow of the most popular of all our wars. One must remember that only thirteen years had elapsed after the signing of the Treaty of Guadalupe Hidalgo when P. G. T. Beauregard, one of the promising young officers who had served with distinction in the army that captured Mexico City,

4

gave the fateful order to fire on Fort Sumter, beginning a war that was destined in time to occupy a pre-eminent place in the American mind and heart.

Still another reason for our apparent indifference to the Mexican War lies rooted in the guilt that we as a nation have come to feel about it. The undeniable fact that it was an offensive war so completely stripped it of moral pretensions that no politician of that era ever succeeded in elevating it to the lofty level of a "crusade." The additional fact that we paid Mexico fifteen million dollars after it was all over—"conscience money," some called it—seemed to confirm the ugliest charges of those who had denounced the war as a cynical, calculated despoiling of the Mexican state, a greedy land-grab from a neighbor too weak to defend herself.

The land hunger was there, to be sure, for expansionism was a dynamic force in America in the 1840's; but there were causes other than greed as there were consequences other than gain. To dismiss the war with Mexico as nothing more than a parade through the chaparral is to lose sight of its broader significance. This small volume will more than adequately serve its intended purpose if it succeeds in conveying to the reader some interest in and appreciation of the wider implications of this unique event that was destined to exert so profound an influence upon the future course of American history.

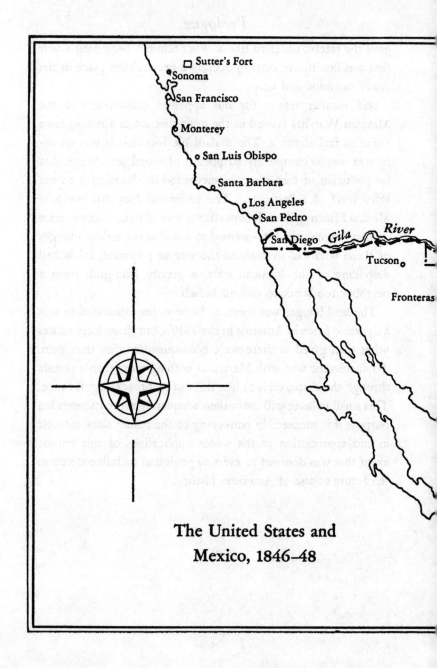

The United States and
Mexico, 1846–48

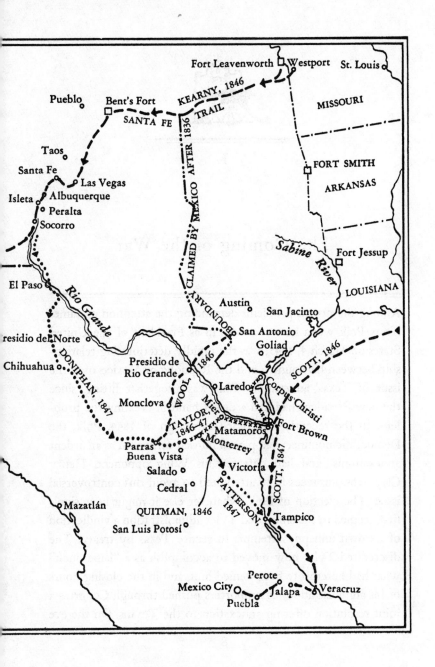

I

The Coming of the War

Among the urgent problems demanding the attention of James Knox Polk when he was sworn in as President of the United States on March 4, 1845, was the rapidly deteriorating relationship between his country and the Republic of Mexico over the issue of Texas' annexation. This was altogether fitting, since the new President had had a direct hand in creating the problem. In the recently concluded campaign of 1844, Polk, the Democratic nominee, had placed himself on record as an ardent annexationist and had defeated his Whig opponent, Henry Clay, who unsuccessfully attempted to avoid this controversial issue. The election of Polk, whatever else it might have signified, seemed to the embattled Tyler administration a vindication of its own unhappy attempts to secure Texas by treaty. The discredited Tyler now moved to accomplish as a "lame duck" what had heretofore been denied him, and in the closing hours of his administration his supporters pushed through Congress a joint resolution offering annexation to the Texans. On the eve of Mr. Polk's inauguration, the outgoing President officially transmitted the offer.

Mexican reaction to this move was instantaneous. The long-smoldering resentment of the Mexicans was fanned into open flames, and talk of war with the United States was heard on all sides. In the meantime, official protests were lodged by the Mexican government questioning both the propriety and the legality of the act. To these protests the United States government repeatedly answered that, aside from all questions of national interest, the right to annex the Republic of Texas, which had won its freedom, maintained its independence, and been officially recognized as a member of the family of nations, was a matter solely between the United States and Texas and that the United States therefore felt no obligation to consult with any other power. Such a reply was in no way satisfactory to Mexico, and toward the end of March, 1845, her minister to the United States demanded his passport and left the country. With the subsequent withdrawal of the American minister to Mexico, the rupture was complete—all diplomatic intercourse between the two nations officially ceased.

In the lull which followed this abrupt and ominous development, both nations turned their attention to Texas. In an effort to thwart the American project, Mexico, encouraged by both England and France, offered recognition to Texas provided the proffered annexation was not consummated. The Texans rejected this Mexican proposal, and, when on July 4, 1845, they formally accepted the United States offer, another wave of indignation swept through Mexico, where sentiment for war had already reached alarming proportions.

As relations between the two countries grew worse, President Polk issued warnings to his military commanders to be prepared for any eventuality. In May, 1845, General Zachary Taylor, the sixty-year-old Indian fighter in command of United States troops in the Southwest, was ordered to hold his forces in readiness, and shortly thereafter the commander of the naval flotilla in Pacific waters, Commodore J. D. Sloat, was instructed to seize ports along the California coast if war should break out. A few weeks later, in response to the angry reaction in Mexico to the annexation of Texas, Polk moved Taylor and his men to Corpus Christi and ordered the navy to assemble the Home Squadron off Mexican ports in the Gulf. Then, in an effort to forestall impending hostilities, the President again resorted to diplomacy. Acting upon the intimated willingness of the Mexican government to receive a representative from this country, Polk dispatched John Slidell as "envoy extraordinary and minister plenipotentiary" to settle outstanding grievances. The mission proved a bootless enterprise, for even as Slidell journeyed southward, pressures within Mexico were brought to bear against the insecure Herrera regime to prevent acceptance of the envoy. Desperately hoping to prevent the fall of his tottering government, José Herrera yielded to the popular clamor and refused to receive Slidell not only on the technical grounds that he had agreed to receive only a "commissioner" but also because acceptance would, in his view, imply the existence of friendly relations between the two countries, which, in turn, could conceivably be misinterpreted as condoning the annexation of Texas. Slidell withdrew to Jalapa to await developments and in March, 1846, was handed his passport.

As it turned out, Herrera's hopes were all in vain, for he was soon overthrown in spite of his rejection of Slidell. A revolution led by General Mariano Paredes erupted in December, 1845, and with popular support succeeded in unseating the hapless Herrera. Paredes was now elevated to the presidency, and, with his inauguration in early January, 1846, all hope of compromise vanished, for his open hostility toward the United States was frequently and forcefully expressed in his repeated public pledges to maintain the boundary line along the Sabine River, separating Texas and Louisiana.

When on January 12, 1846, word reached Washington of the rejection of Slidell and the refusal of Mexico to negotiate, Polk issued the fateful order that set General Taylor in motion. Secretary of War William L. Marcy instructed Taylor to advance to the Rio Grande and take up a defensive position on the east bank of that stream. The General was expressly cautioned not to treat the Mexicans as an "enemy," but he was also authorized to take "appropriate action" should hostilities occur. On the basis of this order Taylor moved out of Corpus Christi and with his little army of less than four thousand men headed southward, preceded by a proclamation written in Spanish and signed by the General, guaranteeing that all civil and religious rights of the inhabitants would be respected and emphasizing his "friendly intentions."

Taylor's movements created great excitement in Mexico City, and Paredes instantly retaliated by ordering Mexican troops northward with instructions to concentrate at Matamoros. This action did nothing to impede the progress of Taylor, and, although Mexican troops were frequently seen in the distance, the American force marched to within fifty miles of Matamoros before being challenged. As Taylor drew up before the Arroyo Colorado, a shallow stream north of the Rio Grande, Mexican troops in his front made preparations to dispute his crossing. A messenger was sent to the American General informing him that any further advance would be considered an act of "open hostility" and that the Mexicans would open fire upon any American attempting to cross that line. Taylor's reply was simply that he intended to cross the stream and that he would open fire if any interference or opposition was offered. As the first detachment of Taylor's force splashed across the arroyo, the Mexicans withdrew without firing a shot. Without further incident, Taylor, in late March, 1846, took up two positions on the upper side of the Rio Grande. He occupied Point Isabel, which, because of its defensive possibilities and adequate anchorage, was selected as his base, and began construction there of Fort Polk. The other spot occupied by Taylor was the area directly across the river from Matamoros, where a fortification was begun that was soon to be named Fort Brown.

In the city across the river, Mexican troops were commanded by General Francisco Mejia, an officer who busied himself in constructing batteries when not engaged in exchanging angry words with Taylor. On the eleventh of April, General Pedro Ampudia, veteran of the Alamo and San Jacinto, bringing three thousand reinforcements with him, assumed command in Matamoros and immediately reversed Mejia's essentially passive policy. In a peremptory message to Taylor, Ampudia ordered him to return to Corpus Christi and gave him twenty-four hours in which to break camp, threatening to begin hostilities if his order was not complied with. Taylor answered by stating that he had been ordered to his present position and there he intended to stay and that while he "regretted" the possibility of war, he would not "avoid" it. He closed his communication by reminding the Mexican leader that responsibility for war would ultimately rest with whoever began it. General Ampudia's ardor apparently cooled upon receipt of Taylor's reply, for the only military activity which ensued was the picking off by Mexican snipers of stragglers from the American camp, which materially increased the mounting tensions between the two forces. At this point, Ampudia was superseded in command by General Mariano Arista, who brought with him additional troops raising the total Mexican forces to approximately eight thousand. Arista assumed command on April 24, 1846, and on the following day sent a sizable cavalry force under Torrejón across the river. Taylor, upon learning of this movement, dispatched a small squadron of dragoons under the command of Captain S. B. Thornton in their direction. Early next morning, the dragoons were surrounded by the Mexicans, and after an unsuccessful attempt to cut their way out they surrendered with the loss of several lives. Here, then, was an overt act of war. No longer could the adversaries pretend that only "irregular forces" were engaged, for Torrejón's attack was carried out by Mexican regulars. As a result of this encounter, General Taylor immediately informed his government that "hostilities may now be considered as commenced" and General Arista was later able to boast: "I had the pleasure of being the first to start the war."

Not until two weeks later did news of the Mexican attack reach Washington. On May 9, after a cabinet meeting in which the issue of war with Mexico had been inconclusively discussed, news of the attack shattered the calm of the capital city. Two days later, the President's war message was read to a tense Congress. The Mexicans, Polk charged, had "shed American blood upon the American soil!" "War exists," he declared, "by the act of Mexico herself." Within two days, both houses of

Congress had approved the war bill authorizing the President to accept fifty thousand volunteers and appropriating ten million dollars for national defense. The war was now official.

Among the claims made and opinions held about the causes of the Mexican War, none has shown more persistence than the glib assertion that the event resulted from the annexation of Texas. This is, of course, gross oversimplification. Annexation was merely the immediate cause of hostilities, the spark that touched off the explosion. Deeper, older, more fundamental causes can be seen in the Mexican resentment which had been created by an aggressive American expansionism, in the hatred engendered in the American heart as a result of Mexican atrocities committed in the barbarous border warfare that had been waged intermittently since the revolt of the Texans, in the almost incredible political instability of the Mexican government, and in the utter failure of diplomacy. All these in one way or another helped set the stage for conflict; annexation was merely the lancing of a festered sore in which a ravaging infection had already done its deadly work.

It would have been hoping for too much to expect Mexico to accept with docility the despoiling of her territory by her land-hungry neighbor. "Manifest Destiny," a euphemism coined by a New York newspaperman for this bumptious expansionism, was a dynamic force in American society, and the penchant of the Yankee for acquiring contiguous territory far antedated the annexation of Texas. Jefferson's purchase of Louisiana, Burr's tangled schemes and impenetrable intrigues, the acquisition of Florida—all were symptoms of the same disease, and long after the guns of the Mexican War were silenced, a rash of filibustering expeditions into Latin America offered irrefutable evidence that the movement had not even then spent its force. By virtue of her geographic proximity to the United States, Mexico was an inevitable target for her acquisitive northern neighbor, and it was only natural that her nationals should be deeply offended by this tendency to absorb her territory. In such a devious way did geography and history conspire to bring on disaster.

This Mexican resentment was, however, a pale thing compared to the hostility many Americans felt toward Mexico, a feeling particularly strong among Texans and their relatives but by no means confined to them. A series of excesses and cruelties running like a red thread through the history of the 1830's and 40's gave rise to this hostility against Mexicans, the intensity of which would be difficult to describe.

The sacking of Zacatecas in retaliation for the revolt which broke out in that area provided ample evidence that not even Mexican nationals could be assured of humane treatment by their government, and the severity of the punishments meted out caused world-wide revulsion. During the Texas Revolution, public opinion in the United States was outraged by two particularly bloody incidents which were the handiwork of General Santa Anna. The slaughter of the tiny garrison defending the Alamo in early March, 1836, and the subsequent burning of their oil-soaked bodies, stacked like cordwood outside the mission, sent a shudder of horror through the American public which not even their pride in the desperate heroism of the defenders could restrain. The pitiless massacre of Texas prisoners at Goliad some three weeks later served only to arouse further American loathing for all things Mexican. James Fannin, in command of Texas forces at Goliad, surrendered to General Urrea with the understanding that his men would be treated as prisoners of war. Santa Anna arbitrarily set aside his subordinate's agreement and ordered the execution of all prisoners, whereupon over three hundred captives were marched outside the town and shot. This hateful policy, epitomized in the Mexican war cry "Exterminate to the Sabine," bore its final bitter fruit in the swamps near the San Jacinto battlefield in April, 1836, when the Texans remorselessly took their revenge on demoralized and defenseless Mexican soldiers who died with the futile protest on their lips, "Me no Alamo, Me no Goliad."

These strong feelings of hostility, generated in the thirties, were carried into and sometimes intensified during the forties. The harsh treatment accorded the prisoners taken from the abortive Santa Fe Expedition, which set out in June of 1841, helped keep alive existing animosities, while Mexican forays into Texas, such as the raid on San Antonio by General Adrian Woll in 1842, tended to aggravate them. In retaliation, a band of Texans invaded Mexico and attacked the town of Mier on Christmas Day, 1842. After exacting a heavy toll from the Mexicans, who were led by the same Ampudia who later commanded Mexican armies in the northern threater of the war, the Texans were forced to surrender, once again with the explicit understanding that they were to be treated as prisoners of war. As the result of an unsuccessful bid to escape, the Texans were ordered to be put to death, although Santa Anna, who was responsible for the order, later changed it to apply only to every tenth man in the group. The victims were selected by drawing colored beans from a jar; the unlucky ones were then blindfolded and shot. Such wanton cruelty had the inevitable effect of creating in the American mind a monstrous anger toward Mexico and Mexicans. In such a milieu of hatred, war fever naturally flourished.

Yet another factor which contributed to the necessity of war was the political instability of the Mexican government. The position of any leader was at best precarious because of a pronounced predilection for revolt, a Spanish inheritance highly refined in Mexican experience. While Spain was engaged in a life-or-death struggle with Napoleon, her grip on the Spanish-American colonies loosened. Mexican political history, beginning with the Hidalgo revolt of 1810, was largely the story of a struggle for independence, culminating in the Iturbide revolt of 1821. The result was the establishment of an independent Mexican empire—an unwieldy creation lasting barely three years.

With the overthrow of that empire in 1824, a republic was proclaimed, but this change in form did nothing to increase stability. There followed a kaleidoscopic rise and fall of governments. The first president, Victoria, was overthrown by his subordinate Guerrero, who was, in turn, overthrown within a year by Bustamante. Thus, within the first half-dozen years of its existence, the republic witnessed the overthrow of its first two executives by the very men who had been elected their vice-presidents. Nor did it end here. This fixed pattern continued through the thirties, into the forties, and, indeed, all during the war. Bustamante was duly deposed in 1832 by Santa Anna, who then dominated the political scene until driven from public office in 1837 by his countrymen for concessions made to the Texans following his disastrous defeat at San Jacinto. Into the resulting political vacuum moved several competing factions. Bustamante enjoyed a temporary revival of power which was ended by a revolt led by Paredes in 1841. The ubiquitous Santa Anna, in a dazzling display of political foot-work, took advantage of the turmoil again to seize power which he held until his exile in 1844. The vacillating Herrera administration retained office during most of 1845, but in the last month of that year was forced out by Paredes, who there-upon assumed personal direction of the affairs of state which he held until after the outbreak of war. In so fluid a situation, it was, perhaps, inevitable that mere survival would become the paramount concern of every regime.

This political instability explains in part why the twenty years of diplomatic intercourse between the United States and Mexico preceding the annexation of Texas were filled with frustration and failure. In 1825, shortly after the republic was proclaimed, the United States sent its first minister, Joel R. Poinsett, to Mexico. His mission was the extremely delicate one of affirming the boundary which had been agreed upon with Spain in the Adams-Onis Treaty of 1819, an assignment which made him *ipso facto* unpopular with the Mexican people. After Bustamante overturned the Guerrero government in 1829, he demanded, as a token gesture to Mexican nationalism, the recall of Poinsett, who thereupon left the country and was eventually replaced by Anthony Butler. Butler's primary achievements were the negotiation in 1832 of a Treaty of Amity and Commerce and a Treaty of Limits, accomplishments which were unfortunately neutralized by his clumsy maneuvers to obtain Texas through what he described as "the influence of money." His blunders led to his recall in 1835, when Powhatan Ellis was named chargé d'affaires.

From the outbreak of the Texas Revolution in 1835, relations between the two countries grew steadily worse. President

The Coming of the War

Jackson's order sending United States troops to the Sabine greatly angered the Mexicans. When, in 1836, the demand of their special envoy, Manuel Gorostiza, for withdrawal of the obnoxious order was refused, that official left the country in a huff. Official recognition of the independence of Texas, announced by the United States on Jackson's last day in office, caused a violent reaction in Mexico that further widened the breach.

In the early forties, tension was heightened by the nagging diplomatic exchange over the Santa Fe prisoners, by frequent raids north of the Rio Grande, and by the Mier expedition. Nor were relations improved by the ill-timed seizure of Monterey Bay by an American naval officer of the Pacific Squadron. In October, 1842, Commodore Thomas Ap Catesby Jones, acting impulsively on an unconfirmed rumor that war between the two countries had actually broken out, forced the surrender of the Mexican garrison and raised the United States flag. Upon discovering to his discomfiture that no war really existed, the Commodore immediately lowered his flag and offered an embarrassed apology to the Mexican government, but little could be done to allay the fear and suspicion which his precipitate action had aroused regarding United States designs on the Mexican province of California.

It was over the question of Texas, however, that the deepest bitterness was stirred, and so keen was Mexican feeling on this particular issue that by the middle of 1843 the Mexican Minister of Foreign Relations flatly warned our resident minister that war would be inevitable if Texas were annexed, a threat that was reiterated in Washington by the Mexican representaitve to the United States. Polk's election on an annexation platform in 1844 was looked upon with unconcealed disfavor in Mexico, and, when annexation was finally consummated, all diplomatic relations with the United States were broken off.

Annexation, then, was one, but by no means the sole, cause of war. The bad feelings that had slowly but surely grown out of the encroachments of one power and the brutalities of the other set the stage for war; political instability increased its probability; the failure of diplomacy made it inevitable.

War, even as it was waged in the middle of the last century, is a vast and complicated enterprise severely taxing the energy and the imagination of those engaged in it. Any nation that hopes to prosecute a war successfully, as indeed warring nations generally do, must face and somehow find solutions for such diverse problems as maintaining unity in support of the war, making correct assumptions about its own power and the relative power of the opposition, organizing and training the necessary military forces, and providing the means, ultimately, for delivering a crushing blow to the enemy. War makes great demands upon a nation, and its eventual outcome is in large measure dependent upon the vision and industry that has gone into the making of basic plans and preparations. Seldom in history have two nations gone to war with such cavalier disregard for realities as did the United States and Mexico in 1846. Indifferent to the staggering problems that faced them, innocent of having conceived even the most elementary plan of campaign, wholly unprepared, each country entered the conflict with an enormously exaggerated view of its own strength and with a feeling of contempt for the other.

In Mexico, there was widespread belief, even as war moved closer, that the United States would not willingly fight. This consoling view, long and lovingly held by many important

Mexicans, was supported by an imposing array of arguments, chief among them being the well-known military weakness of the United States, the vulnerability of American shipping, the immorality and injustice of such a war, and the internal dissensions over slavery and tariff which made any kind of unity seemingly impossible. And even should an awareness of these handicaps fail to restrain the United States, there were reassuring indications that in any war between the two nations, Mexico would enjoy tremendous advantages. For one thing, her armed forces appeared to be in superb condition. Her artillerymen and European-trained engineers were highly regarded in military circles and her numerous infantry units were officered by the flower of Mexican society. The cavalry, most popular of all Mexican military forces, numbered in its ranks horsemen who yielded to none in skill and grace. These impressive forces were further blessed by the advantages which always accrue to the defensive power: interior lines, the use of fortifications, thorough knowledge of the terrain, and general control of time and place of battle.

The international situation, as interpreted by the Mexicans, also buttressed their faith in Mexico's superiority should war come. It was commonly believed in Mexico that European intervention and support would be immediately forthcoming in case of war. This belief was based upon the assumption that the fear and jealousy which European powers, especially England and France, felt toward the United States would leave them no alternative. These various beliefs combined to produce in the Mexican mind a feeling of security, even of smugness, as the threat of war grew daily more serious.

It soon became obvious, however, that the Mexicans greatly overrated their advantages. Disunited, torn with factionalism, rotten with corruption and nearly bankrupt, the government of Mexico proved unequal to the huge tasks imposed by war. Her vaunted military machine was vastly overrated. The ineffectiveness of the artillery was appalling, and the cavalry proved too light to absorb the bruising shock of the charges hurled against it. Indeed, the entire army was vitiated by the flaws inherent in the Mexican military system, a system properly belonging to the eighteenth century, when aristocratic officers commanded soldiers from the depressed classes. The infantry, recruited from the offscourings of society, was commanded by men who frequently were ignorant of the military profession, incompetents who held their positions through favor or intrigue or both. Everywhere there was a shortage of arms and equipment, and there was no industrial plant in Mexico capable of producing them. Mexican seapower, furthermore, was a fiction.

These internal weaknesses were compounded by serious mistakes in judging the outside world. Mexican confidence in the inevitability of foreign intervention turned out to be a disastrous misjudgment, one matched only by Mexican miscalculation of the American temper. They completely failed to anticipate the temporary unity of action that the declaration of war made possible.

Equally serious were the misconceptions being circulated north of the Rio Grande. The American people have historically been overconfident of victory, and the Mexican War was no exception to this tradition. The careless contempt of the Anglo-Saxon for "inferiors," sharpened by revulsion against Mexican brutalities and reinforced by an unfaltering belief in the superiority of his own military prowess, made it easy for the average American to accept the popular assertion that one great thrust was all that would be required to end the war.

The Coming of the War

There was, of course, little basis for such easy optimism. Though few Americans were willing to face them, the problems of waging offensive war against Mexico were staggering. The great distances involved, the rugged and forbidding mountain ranges, the problem of subsisting an army on arid desert terrain, and the ever present danger of attack by that most deadly and dependable of Mexican allies, yellow fever, presented difficulties of no small dimensions. Then, too, the obvious lack of national unity was bound to have an adverse effect on the war effort. The most determined opposition came from New England abolitionists who saw in the war a gigantic and devious plot to insure the spread of slavery, but there was also a noticeable lack of enthusiasm on the part of influential members of the Whig party who disliked Mr. Tyler and distrusted his successor. After an initial wave of enthusiasm, opposition to the administration began to coalesce, and the charge was frequently repeated that there had, in reality, not been sufficient provocation for such extreme action. This opposition, further disgruntled by the onerous taxes that were levied, began openly and unreservedly to condemn the causes, conduct, and consequences of what was fashionably referred to as "Mr. Polk's War."

Another obstacle to successful prosecution of the war was the lack of co-ordination between foreign policy and military policy. Few nations have equaled the United States in so recklessly inviting destruction by ignoring the need for some semblance of balance in this important area. In the 1830's and 40's we were pursuing a most aggressive foreign policy with regard to both Texas and Oregon. Such a course by its very nature entailed great risks. Yet at the same time, when our foreign policy threatened to embroil us not in one but quite possibly in two wars, we were pursuing a casual, weak, even negligent military policy. At a moment when war with England and/or Mexico was imminent, the United States had less than seven thousand men under arms. When war finally came, Congress was busily engaged in a debate over whether or not the military academy at West Point should be abolished! This schism in national policy could have but one result. Consequently, in spite of United States superiority in naval power and industrial capacity, our military prospects were far from encouraging. The small regular force, in which over a third of the soldiers were foreign-born, was wholly inadequate. Except for Indian campaigns, there had been no war since 1812, and the troops, having served most of their time in scattered frontier garrisons, were unacquainted with the intricacies of military maneuver.

Thus, the two nations drifted into war. Mexico, for her part, entered the struggle heavily laden with burdens of her own creation. Even before her troops crossed the Rio Grande, she had been made vulnerable by virtue of having underestimated the power of her adversary, of having seriously miscalculated her own strength and having completely misread the international scene. The United States, on the other hand, apparently oblivious to the inadequacy of her military force, unperturbed by the serious threat of internal division and indifferent to the calamitous effects of a disjointed policy, entered lightly into the war with scarcely a thought of the monumental problems involved.

Washington in the spring of 1846 was the scene of feverish activity as the Polk administration hastily and belatedly, began to make plans for the war which had just been officially declared. If American military history taught no other lesson, it would still be worth studying because it so clearly underscores the fact that we are a people upon whom the gods have smiled. How else can the remarkable fact be explained that we have so often escaped the destruction which our own blunders and stupidities seemed to invite? Fully half a dozen times in our history we have gone into a war for which we were totally unprepared—each time managing to survive while hastily forging a military machine and, miraculously enough, each time attaining victory. The Mexican War was yet another example of the national preference for a policy of "hurry up and catch up."

During the week following receipt of the news of the outbreak of hostilities, the administration in Washington was steeped in planning. Faced suddenly with the ugly reality of war, the President and his cabinet members were forced to give immediate consideration to such urgent needs as selecting a strategic plan, raising the necessary manpower, and performing the other countless chores essential to victory.

With the aid of General Winfield Scott, Polk and his advisers speedily decided upon a plan of operation involving both invasion and blockade. Two overland routes were selected: one toward Monterrey, Saltillo, San Luis Potosí, and central Mexico and the other westward into New Mexico, Chihuahua, and California. Both movements were hastily conceived, and very little thought was given to such important matters as the condition of roads, the availability of water, or transportation and supplies for the army. Simultaneously, orders were issued by the Navy Department to blockade Veracruz and other ports in the Gulf of Mexico.

Having made these basic strategic decisions, attention was

next focused on the problem of raising troops. Based on an estimation that, in addition to the regular army, 25,000 men were needed immediately, steps were taken to fill these billets by means of federal requisitions on the states. Because of their proximity to the enemy, the states in the south and southwest were called upon to provide the 25,000 urgently needed troops. A quota of 40,000 troops was levied among the rest of the states with the understanding that these would be made available for duty when the government should require their services. The twelve-month enlistment of volunteers was in keeping with the widespread optimism that the war would be over in a relatively short time.

Meanwhile, the administration maintained a conciliatory attitude toward the enemy and thereby kept open the possibility of renewing negotiations. General Taylor was instructed to follow a policy of leniency toward the enemy in his forward movements and to try to win acceptance by the Mexican population in any area he might occupy.

Perhaps the most far-fetched and certainly the most ridiculous scheme hatched by the planners in Washington was their attempt to secure peace with Mexico by conniving to restore Santa Anna to power. The General's erratic political career had once again been interrupted when in 1844 he was deposed and subsequently banished. His exile was spent in Havana, where for eighteen months he divided his time between two favorite Latin pastimes, cockfighting and political intrigue. President Polk had several reasons for thinking that Santa Anna's restoration might mean the return of peace—not the least among them being the assurances of a confidant of the General to that effect. At any rate, in an effort to facilitate Santa Anna's return, Polk asked his Secretary of the Navy, George Bancroft, to notify the American naval commander in the Gulf that if the General made any attempt to enter a Mexican port, he was to be allowed to "pass freely." Shortly thereafter, an emissary, Alexander Slidell Mackenzie, a naval officer who had attained notoriety in 1842 for having hanged the son of the Secretary of War for an attempted mutiny aboard Mackenzie's ship, the "Somers," was dispatched from Washington. Mackenzie, who spoke Spanish fluently, journeyed to Cuba ostensibly to investigate a report that privateers were being outfitted there. Nevertheless, he conveniently found time for a lengthy visit with the exiled Mexican leader.

Santa Anna evidently played his cards extremely well, for Polk remained unshaken in his faith in the soundness of this plan. The overthrow of Paredes early in August, 1846, was the signal Santa Anna had been awaiting, and on the sixteenth he made a triumphant entry into Mexico, landing at Veracruz without hindrance from United States naval forces. Within a month Santa Anna was once again given command of the Mexican army, a position from which he moved with energy to organize and train a force to defeat the advancing North Americans. Whatever results President Polk might have been expecting, there is no escaping the ironic fact that his ultimate achievement was to have aided in placing in command of the enemy's army the most competent soldier in their service. The price for this amateurish dabbling was soon paid in American lives on the battlefield at Buena Vista and in numerous bloody encounters fought along the road to Mexico City.

II

The Invasion of Northern Mexico

Within a few days after the defeat of Thornton in late April, 1846, General Arista crossed the Rio Grande below Matamoros and led his army onto soil claimed by the United States. General Taylor, realizing that his position at Fort Brown was now vulnerable and that this Mexican force might easily cut him off from his base at Point Isabel, determined to return to the coast and personally oversee the construction of defenses there. Accordingly, on the afternoon of May 1, leaving a garrison of five hundred men under Major Brown to defend the fort, Taylor set the remainder of his small army in motion toward the seacoast, and by noon on the following day the twenty-six-mile march was completed without incident.

The ensuing five days were devoted to the improvement of defenses at Fort Polk, and, since the troops were employed as working parties, they were happy to complete this onerous chore and rejoin their comrades at Fort Brown. On May 7, Taylor, with slightly more than two thousand troops followed by an immense baggage train, began to retrace his steps. Arista had already decided to intercept Taylor on his return trip.

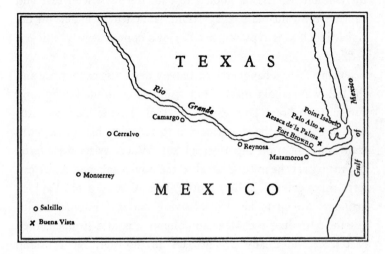

OPERATIONS IN TEXAS AND NORTHERN MEXICO

While waiting for the Americans to move, the Mexican commander devoted his time to shelling the garrison inside Fort Brown. Upon receipt of the news that Taylor was again en route, Arista moved out to meet him, assuming a defensive position near the watering hole of Palo Alto. There, in the early afternoon of May 8, Taylor encountered the enemy, six thousand strong, drawn up across the road in battle array, obviously intending to dispute his advance. Delaying only long enough to fill canteens and water horses, Taylor hastened to attack. The battle opened about three o'clock in the afternoon with an artillery duel that lasted for more than an hour. The Mexican pieces were surprisingly ineffective. Their fire was generally inaccurate and so deficient were they in range that the balls frequently fell short and bounced along the ground so that American troops could actually dodge them. Following the cannonade, Arista, hoping to gain the American rear and capture the valuable baggage train, launched an attack on the right which was repulsed by Taylor's comparatively efficient artillery.

During this exchange, the extremely dry grass caught fire and the billowing smoke made it impossible to continue the fighting for fully an hour. During this interval, Taylor used the protective cover of the smoke screen to redeploy his forces, concentrating them on the Mexican left. When Arista discovered this maneuver, he in turn attacked the now weakened American left, threatening Taylor's entire line. Once again Taylor's artillery proved to be the decisive element, for under its incessant pounding the Mexican column was first stopped, then shattered, and finally driven back in disorder. No crushing blow was delivered, however, because the rapidly approaching darkness and the vulnerability of his baggage train prevented Taylor's following up his advantage. Thus ended the first regular engagement in the war with Mexico. After losing over two hundred men, nearly four times as many as the Americans, the Mexican army had been driven from the field.

Early next morning, May 9, Arista began to retreat to a stronger position and by mid-morning had arrived at the Resaca de la Guerrero, a dried-up riverbed offering attractive defensive possibilities. Placing his troops behind the natural fortifications thus offered, in a spot so thickly covered with chaparral that the enemy's troublesome artillery would be effectively neutralized, Arista had ample reason to feel that his position was secure and that his superior numbers would now prove decisive. Taylor, after caring for his wounded, moved forward in pursuit of the retreating Mexicans and in the early afternoon called a halt at the Resaca de la Palma to allow his foot soldiers to rest while his scouts sought out the enemy. About two o'clock, the main force was again set in motion when Taylor received a report on the location of the Mexican army.

After reconnoitering the Mexican position, Taylor determined upon a frontal assault, since no flanking movement was possible. The first attack was made by the hard-riding dragoons, who struck the right wing of the Mexican line with great force and captured several guns. Taking advantage of the confusion thus created, Taylor hurriedly sent his infantry charging into the fray, and in the brush-fighting which followed, the wildest disorder prevailed; officers and men lost all contact, friend and foe were closely intermingled, and in the hand-to-hand combat which raged in that quarter, the bayonet was freely used. Shortly after five o'clock, Arista's right wing completely collapsed. His line reeled backward under the pressure of the American attack, and the retreat turned into a rout as his disorganized soldiers fled in the direction of the river they had recently crossed. As the Mexicans, in their headlong dash toward the protective works at Matamoros, passed under the guns of Fort Brown, they were further harassed by a biting fire from the jubilant garrison.

At the Battle of the Resaca, the Americans were again victorious; nearly 1,200 Mexicans had been killed or wounded, while their own loss was only 150 men. General Arista had not even enjoyed the privilege of witnessing the greater part of the battle. When the engagement began, he was working in his tent, and, thinking the firing signified nothing more than a skirmish, he conscientiously continued his writing. By the time he realized his mistake, it was too late to salvage a victory. In fact, so hasty was the retreat that even the General's personal baggage had to be abandoned, and when the Yankees ransacked his private papers, they discovered, much to their delight, an order from the Mexican government directing Arista to send General Taylor to Mexico City as a prisoner.

While the Battles of Palo Alto and the Resaca were being fought, Fort Brown was also being subjected to a steady bombardment. In fact, during the entire week from the third to the ninth of May, this relentless shelling continued without any real opposition from the defenders, who were carefully hoarding their small store of ammunition in order to repel any enemy assault. On the sixth of May, Major Brown was killed, but even then no attempt was made to storm the fort, and after Arista's main army had been hurled back across the river, Taylor re-entered the fort. When the damage had been surveyed, Taylor made another quick trip to Point Isabel, bringing back with him enough supplies and reinforcements to support his impending move against the enemy now intrenched at Matamoros.

By the seventeenth of the month, all was in readiness for an attack on the city. Arista had received orders to hold Matamoros as long as possible, but in view of the low morale of his twice-defeated troops and the lukewarm support of his officers, he decided to evacuate the city rather than engage his adversary again. To stall for time, he sent an emissary to Taylor to enter into a prolonged discussion of truce terms while he hurriedly moved as many guns and supplies from the city as he could. From Matamoros, Arista moved to Linares, where he arrived near the end of May only to find awaiting him a set of orders relieving him of his command.

On the eighteenth of May, the American army jubilantly

occupied Matamoros without opposition, and certainly there was cause for their rejoicing. On consecutive days they had twice defeated an enemy three times their number in pitched battles that not only increased prestige abroad but also created satisfaction at home, where the populace had already begun to mention Zachary Taylor's name in connection with a certain high office. Moreover, the acknowledged superiority of American artillery and the demonstrated ability of the American soldier in close combat had a buoyant effect upon the army, instilling it with that aggressive self-confidence which is indispensable to high morale. To top it all, they had pressured a numerically superior enemy into abandoning a well-fortified city without so much as a token resistance. Small wonder, then, at the undisguised elation that was expressed as the American flag was raised, and an American army officer assumed the duties of military governor of Matamoros, thereby making that border town the first Mexican city to undergo the transforming experience of Americanization through occupation.

In 1846, Monterrey was a city of nearly fifteen thousand inhabitants situated on the important thoroughfare that cut through the mountains at Rinconada Pass, between Monterrey and Saltillo. Strategically, it was the key point in the northern Mexican theater of operations and was, therefore, of tremendous importance to both antagonists. That the Mexicans appreciated its importance was attested to by the fact that Mejia, after having superseded Arista in command, was ordered to concentrate his forces there and to make every preparation for the defense of the city against the invaders. Its possession was deemed equally important by the United States not only because its capture was in keeping with the basic aim to carry on offensive war in that region but also to give an added measure of security to the Rio Grande area and to provide another anchor for the defensive line being set up across northern Mexico.

In the first week in June of 1846, Taylor began his advance from Matamoros toward Monterrey. Moving up the south bank of the Rio Grande he occupied Reynosa before moving on to Camargo, a town of some five thousand inhabitants located near the San Juan River where it empties into the Rio Grande. There he remained in camp for nearly six weeks gathering supplies and fighting off the diseases which, according to one soldier, had converted the place into "a Yawning Graveyard." Finally in the middle of August, having collected a vast amount of supplies, Taylor moved on to occupy Cerralvo. By the seventeenth of September he was at Marín, last stop along the road to Monterrey. Early in the morning of the nineteenth, the American army arrived on the outskirts of the city they intended to capture, and Taylor set up his headquarters in a pleasant grove known as the Wood of San Domingo, supremely confident that his army of six thousand men was up to the task of taking the city "pretty much with the bayonet."

Within Monterrey, meanwhile, preparations continued apace. Reinforcements sent by the Mexican government brought the total number of troops in the city to above seven thousand by mid-September, and the crafty Ampudia, whose persistent plottings to secure high command had finally borne fruit, had now assumed personal direction of preparations for defense. Immediately after replacing Mejia, the new commander placed the city under strict martial law and concentrated on the construction of fortifications.

The afternoon of the nineteenth was spent in reconnoitering the city, and the report of its defenses which the engineers brought in would have given pause to a less determined man than Taylor. The natural setting of Monterrey made it easily defensible. Nested among the foothills of the Sierra Madre Range, the city had grown up on the north bank of the Santa Catarina River. The rear of the town was protected by a series of hills which made attack from that direction most unlikely.

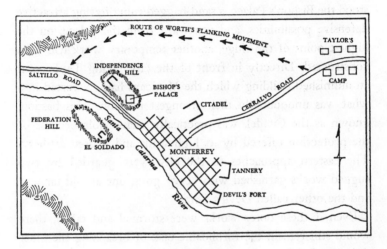

MONTERREY

On the west, the important road from Rinconada Pass and Saltillo entered the city between two commanding heights: south of the river lay Federation Hill while to the north rose Independence Hill. The northern and eastern approaches to the city were comparatively open, and in these areas the Mexicans had dug a network of ditches and constructed a series of defensive works. By thus taking advantage of the natural defenses and augmenting them with man-made ones, the Mexicans had transformed Monterrey into a fortress city.

An arc-shaped outer ring of defenses added greatly to the

strength of the city. The river and mountains in the rear removed the need for any formidable positions in that area, but in all other directions imposing works had been completed. On the west, both major heights were strongly fortified. On Federation Hill, a stone fort known as El Soldado had been erected, and further to the west, on the crest of the hill, an earthwork had been thrown up. Across the Saltillo Road on Independence Hill stood the Bishop's Palace, a sand-bagged ruin offering attractive defensive possibilities, and westward from the palace, on the highest point of the ridge, another temporary work had been constructed. Directly in front of the city facing Taylor was an unfinished building which the Mexicans had converted into what was undoubtedly their strongest position. This bastion, known as the Citadel, was practically unassailable because of the protection offered by its high walls and massed artillery. The eastern approaches to the city were guarded by two rugged works garnished with heavy guns, one an old tannery and the other called Devil's Fort.

Even if these outer works were stormed and taken, there would still remain the formidable task of breaching the inner defenses. Stone houses loop-holed for snipers, flat roofs with sandbag parapets, and barricaded streets gave the city the appearance of impregnability. In front of the Americans, then, was a city of stone protected by numerous and well-constructed fortifications, abundantly supplied with ammunition and provisions, and defended by a force larger than anything the invaders could hope to muster.

Following the afternoon reconnaissance of the nineteenth, Taylor called his officers into a council of war to discuss the best means of taking the city. Out of this conference came the basic tactical decision that largely determined how the Battle of Monterrey would be fought: it was imperative to gain possession of the Saltillo Road, the main artery for bringing in Mexican supplies and reinforcements and the only path for their possible retreat, before attempting an assault on the city itself. In order to carry out this plan, Taylor, in violation of the principle of concentration, deliberately divided his force in the face of a superior enemy and sent General William Jenkins Worth, with two thousand men, on a flanking movement to the west while he, Taylor, remained in front of the city with the main body of his army. Thus, the assault on Monterrey was to be a two-pronged drive with Worth moving in from the west and Taylor moving directly against the town.

Sunday, September 20, was essentially a day of maneuver. At about two o'clock in the afternoon, Worth moved off to the right intent on carrying out his orders to turn Independence Hill, occupy the Saltillo highway, and capture any works that impeded his progress. Most of the afternoon was spent in this movement, though by six o'clock Worth had approached near enough to the Saltillo Road to be challenged by a body of Mexican troops. With darkness closing in, Worth wisely determined to wait until morning to make his bid.

While Worth was moving toward his objective, Taylor maintained an annoying bombardment on the opposite end of the town and had actually made several feints with his infantry in order to prevent Mexican reinforcements being sent against Worth. With Taylor in front and Worth on the flank, the stage was now set for the fierce three-day battle that followed.

During the night a heavy rain began to fall, and, when Worth resumed his movement early next morning, the darkness and the drizzling rain provided so effective a cover that he was not detected until he had nearly reached the road. The furious charge of the Mexicans was broken by the deadly fire of his men, and, after forcing their retreat, Worth by eight o'clock that morning had seized the Saltillo Road, all-important lifeline for the defenders in the city.

At this juncture, the advancing Americans came under the fire of enemy works on both Federation and Independence Hills, and it was soon clear that these two positions would have to be taken before any serious advance could be made against Monterrey. By noon, Worth was ready to advance against Federation Hill, which he proposed to take first. After fording the shallow Santa Catarina, the American troops drove in the enemy pickets, charged up the slope, and in a short but sharp struggle wrested the earthwork from its defenders, who now fell back on El Soldado. Assaulting this fort was a larger order, however, and some delay was occasioned while Worth sent up additional men and heavier guns. After hurling an artillery barrage into the work, the infantry were sent against it and attacked with a fury that sent the Mexicans fleeing into Monterrey. The capture of El Soldado meant that Federation Hill was now entirely in American hands and that the major threat to their advance in that quarter was removed. Across the road, however, forbidding in appearance, stood Independence Hill, and from the Bishop's Palace and the western redoubt a galling fire was kept up against the Americans. Since it was now late afternoon and his troops were weary from the day's activities, Worth decided to wait until morning to attack this formidable height.

While Worth was thus engaged on the flank, Taylor had continued activities in his quarter designed to compel Ampudia to keep heavy forces concentrated on his front. As Worth moved toward the Saltillo Road, Taylor made several feints, all the while continuing to throw shells into the city. Later in the day, he actually launched a series of assaults and his infantry, keeping safely out of range of the guns of the Citadel, struck on the eastern edge of town. In the close fighting that followed, such heavy losses were inflicted on the attackers that they were withdrawn late in the afternoon, yielding all the ground taken that day except the tannery, which they had seized and garrisoned. The fighting on the eastern flank that fateful Monday was fierce and costly; more American lives were lost here than at any other time in the three-day contest and with no compensating gain.

The rain continued, and Worth's cold and hungry men spent another miserable night in the open. Next morning, Tuesday, September 22, reveille sounded at 3 A.M., and Worth, again taking advantage of the cover afforded by the weather, ordered his men to advance quietly upon Independence Hill. A misty fog muffled the noises of the advancing troops, and, since the darkness blanketed them from view, they very nearly gained the top of the hill before being detected by enemy sentries. As soon as the alarm was sounded, the Americans dashed toward the temporary work that had been constructed there and after a short struggle succeeded in driving the Mexicans out. Before dawn, then, the invaders had seized the westernmost redoubt, but as daylight improved visibility, they could see clearly, down the slope, the guns of the heavily fortified Bishop's Palace trained directly upon them. The remainder of the morning was spent in bringing up heavy guns and placing them in position to shell the palace. After this tedious work was completed, a lengthy artillery duel took place as the adversaries tried to blast one another out of position. By lobbing howitzer shells into the roofless palace, the Americans caused such damage that the Mexicans were compelled to launch a sortie in an effort to drive them from their position. Their courageous advance against the entrenched Americans was stopped cold, and as the Mexicans began their retreat, the invaders unleashed an attack that swept everything before it. The palace was quickly taken, and as the Mexicans fled pell-mell into the city, their own captured guns were turned upon their rear from the hill. Thus, by four o'clock in the afternoon of the twenty-second, the palace was taken; Worth was now in possession of the western approaches to the city. The Mexican line of retreat or reinforcement was cut, and Worth was now free to move directly against the town from the west. As the American flag was raised atop the ruined Bishop's Palace, Taylor's soldiers, who had been anxiously watching from the east, gave a shout of joy that must have warmed the hearts of Worth's weary campaigners.

Taylor had, meanwhile, remained comparatively inactive, resting his men after their exertions of the day before, but throughout the day he continued bombarding the city. During the night, Ampudia ordered his outer works abandoned, except the Citadel which he correctly considered impregnable, and concentrated his forces in the inner ring of defenses.

At daybreak on the morning of the twenty-third, Taylor again began an advance into the city from the northeast, and any depression his troops might have felt because of the dismal rainy weather which plagued their progress was dispelled upon discovering that Monterrey's defenders had abandoned their strong outer works. When he had occupied and garrisoned these, Taylor ordered his troops on, and by ten in the morning they were fighting in the streets and houses of Monterrey.

Worth had remained idle during the morning, awaiting instructions from his superior. When the firing in the town finally convinced him that an assault was under way, he began to advance along the two roads leading into the city from the Bishop's Palace. By midday, the Americans were closing in from two directions. Mexican resistance continued, however, and the afternoon was spent in house-by-house and hand-to-hand street fighting. Using crowbars, axes, and battering rams, the Americans burrowed through walls and came up behind Mexican sharpshooters on the flat-roofed houses. By the time darkness fell, both Taylor and Worth had moved relentlessly nearer the heart of the city and were in position to shell the arsenal which Ampudia had established in the cathedral.

On the following morning, the American forces resumed their burrowing, but before any serious engagement could begin, Ampudia, fearful of an explosion in his magazine, sent an aide under a flag of truce to propose terms under which the city might be yielded to the Americans. Taylor, in reply, demanded unconditional surrender and gave the Mexican general until noon to answer. Ampudia then countered with a request for an interview, and the problem was finally resolved by the appointment of a joint commission to consider terms. After lengthy deliberation, the commissioners agreed upon immediate surrender of the town, transference of all public property therein to the Americans, and retirement of all Mexican forces beyond Rinconada Pass. In addition, an eight weeks' armistice was proclaimed with the stipulation that either government reserved the right to veto this agreement made in the field.

Such lenient terms granted a surrendering enemy were justified not only by Taylor's expressed wish to prevent further bloodshed and to restore amicable relations between the two warring nations but by military considerations as well. The Mexicans were still intrenched in formidable positions that would undoubtedly have to be taken by assault, a feat that would have been difficult if not impossible for Taylor's fatigued army, now dangerously low on ammunition and provisions. At any rate, Mexican troops evacuated the Citadel on Friday, September 25, and during the following days moved out of the city with Ampudia under an escort of regular officers of the United States Army which he had requested for his personal protection until he had moved beyond reach of the Texans. Monterrey was immediately occupied by the American army that had paid five hundred lives for the privilege.

The successful conclusion of the campaign against Monterrey was of considerable significance because of its impact upon the political as well as the military situation. Worth, because of his brilliant flanking movement, emerged with increased stature. His reputation among the soldiers was greatly enhanced, and there was more than a little justification for the feeling, expressed by one of the officers, that Worth was now "the high comb cock" of the army. But it was Taylor who profited most from the affair. His popularity was immeasurably increased, not only among the troops, who admired his tenacity, but also among the folks back home. Appropriately embellished stories were beginning to be circulated that not only flattered the General's vanity but also kept his political star on the rise. The victory also provided another boost for the army's morale. At relatively small cost, they had wrested from the enemy a strategically located, heavily fortified city and captured guns, ammunition, and valuable stores.

The Invasion of Northern Mexico

For the small American army, it had truly been, in General Scott's words, "three glorious days."

After the capture of Monterrey, Taylor remained in the city making plans for future operations. As his political ambitions blossomed, he grew increasingly suspicious of the motives of the Polk administration. This suspicion, combined with the General's natural bluntness and taciturnity, led inevitably to friction. When Taylor received the unwelcome order directing him to terminate the armistice he had only recently negotiated, he became furious. Yet, in spite of this open repudiation, he dutifully notified his adversary of the government's decision. Taylor, grumbling all the while about political persecution, turned his attention to further offensive operations. Having decided that his next move should be the occupation of Saltillo, the important and relatively unprotected city that commanded the western approaches to Rinconada Pass, Taylor, on the same morning that he received word from his worried government not to attempt to hold territory beyond Monterrey, sent Worth marching toward Saltillo. On the sixteenth of November, Worth occupied Saltillo, and Taylor established his own headquarters on a site beyond the town.

Meanwhile, other campaigns, reflecting the desire of the administration to occupy territory in northern Mexico, were being carried out. One of these was an expedition against Tampico, a major seaport on the Gulf that was not only the most important city in the state of Tamaulipas but also one that could be used as a base from which to move against enemy forces in the interior. No real resistance ever materialized. Commodore P. S. P. Conner, in compliance with orders directing him to attack the city, sent a flotilla to batter it into submission only to discover that the Mexicans, without attempting to hold the position, had withdrawn. On the fifteenth of November, Tampico was officially occupied, and within a short time a garrison was established.

Another of these peripheral operations was General Wool's expedition against Chihuahua. John E. Wool, a regular army officer who was something of a martinet, had been ordered to conduct this operation to detach Chihuahua and threaten Durango and so to add another link to the chain of defensive posts held by American troops in northern Mexico. When his force was assembled at San Antonio, Wool began his advance in late September and by the eighth of October had reached the Rio Grande. At this point, Wool, upon receiving the intelligence that Santa Anna was gathering a large force at San Luis Potosí with which to move against Taylor, abandoned the original plan to move against Chihuahua and decided instead to move to some point where he might readily reinforce Taylor if needed. Moving due south, he occupied Monclova and after a short stay there moved on to set up headquarters in Parras in early December. Two weeks later, on orders from Taylor, Wool marched to join the main American army, arriving at Worth's camp near Saltillo on the twenty-first of December. The long march from San Antonio was of no military significance in itself, yet Wool's appearance at Saltillo did bring valuable reinforcements to Taylor in time for the showdown fight with Santa Anna that was to be the greatest single battle of the entire war.

By the end of 1846, then, almost all of northeastern Mexico was in American hands. United States troops were garrisoned in Matamoros, Reynosa, Camargo, Monterrey, Saltillo, and Tampico—the foremost cities in the states of Tamaulipas, Nuevo León, and Coahuila. And as these successful operations had progressed, they had unavoidably brought to a head that perplexing strategic question of what should be done next. Among the influential men surrounding the President, there was considerable interest in an essentially defensive policy of merely holding what had already been taken from Mexico, thereby shifting to the enemy the burden of waging offensive war. Taylor, himself, advocated holding such a defensive line, though his support of this plan was generated by a belief that, because of the desert and the immense distances involved, it would be sheer folly to attempt an invasion of central Mexico from the north.

The administration in Washington, however, remained justifiably suspicious of this defensive policy. Impressed with the necessity for striking a blow at the enemy's vitals in order to offset the growing unpopularity of the war on the home front and convinced that carrying the war to the Mexican people would exert great influence in bringing about negotiations for peace, the political leaders settled upon an offensive plan. In October, 1846, Polk, on the advice of his cabinet, made the basic decision to move against Mexico City by way of Veracruz. Agreeing on the impracticability of an advance toward San Luis Potosí from the north and fearing that further advances from that direction were actually dangerous, Polk sent a message to Taylor instructing him to confine his operations within the limits of the Monterrey line.

Following a short but agonizing period of indecision, Polk reluctantly named General Winfield Scott to command the Veracruz expedition. Scott subsequently notified Taylor that, in order to insure the success of this new venture, many of Taylor's troops would be needed. Scott further informed Taylor that he was merely to hold the line already established.

The Mexican War

The disgruntled Taylor, nursing yet another grudge against superiors who seemed to him industriously plotting his downfall, re-established his headquarters at Monterrey and began concentrating troops for Scott while bringing to a conclusion the movement against Ciudad Victoria, which was occupied in January, 1847.

In that same month, General Scott arrived in the northern theater of operations and began collecting troops for the proposed movement against the Mexican capital. While in the area, Scott's dealings with Taylor, who studiously avoided a meeting with his superior officer, were remarkably considerate. But as he prepared to leave the area, Scott hopelessly alienated Taylor by repeating emphatically the order for Taylor to remain strictly on the defensive.

Convinced that the administration was scheming to disgrace him and spurred on by the haunting fear of political eclipse, the hard-headed and embittered soldier now deliberately disobeyed orders. In spite of the government's instructions not to move in force beyond Monterrey and in spite of General Scott's positive order to remain on the defensive, Taylor, with unconcealed petulance, moved his force beyond Saltillo and in early February, 1847, took up an advanced position at Agua Nueva some twenty miles south of the city. This act undoubtedly gave him great personal satisfaction; it also left him open to the charge of insubordination.

While these events were taking place in the northern theater of war, Santa Anna had not remained inactive. Since he had been allowed by American authorities to return to his homeland, the wily Mexican lost no time in showing that he had no real intentions of working for peace but, rather, intended to capitalize on the situation to increase his own power. After landing at Veracruz, he made his way slowly to Mexico City. There he used his immense energies to consolidate his political power before departing to assume the field command that had been tendered him. On the twenty-eigth of September, 1846, Santa Anna left the capital and headed for San Luis Potosí, intending to organize a massive force for the victory he so desperately needed to bolster his sagging fortunes.

In spite of public hostility, troublesome personal problems, and pressing financial difficulties, Santa Anna succeeded in raising an army of twenty-five thousand men. As he was training this force, one of those minor incidents occurred which often change the face of war. In early January, 1847, his scouts brought in a letter from Scott to Taylor which they had intercepted. This captured dispatch told all; it not only informed Santa Anna of the proposed expedition against Veracruz but also provided an accurate count of the troops left under Taylor's command. This welcome intelligence meant that Santa Anna now had a choice of action: he could either move to Veracruz and prepare a warm reception for Scott, or he could hurry to the north and attack Taylor in his now weakened condition. After a careful weighing of possibilities, Santa Anna, convinced that the opportunity for a smashing victory was greater in the north, decided to strike Taylor. Certain that the fortress in the harbor at Veracruz could hold out for a time and confident that he could destroy Taylor with one crushing blow, the Mexican commander eagerly headed his army northward on the second day of February, 1847.

The march from San Luis Potosí was a terrible experience for the Mexican army. In the desert country they crossed, water was scarce, food was in short supply, and the winter weather was unusually severe. Yet in spite of sickness and exposure and the increasing number of desertions that plagued him, Santa Anna arrived on the twenty-first of February at La Encarnación, almost two hundred miles from his point of origin, still in command of an army numbering twenty thousand men.

Taylor was at first reluctant to believe that Santa Anna was moving against him in force. Earliest scouting reports were either discounted or entirely dismissed by the American commander who had eagerly taken the bait expertly proferred by Santa Anna—a deliberately misleading circular announcing the intention of the Mexican commander to move his main force to Veracruz. However, as intelligence reports continued to warn of a large force moving toward the north, Taylor became more concerned. Aware that his position at Agua Nueva could be easily turned in either direction by the enemy, Taylor dispatched reliable Ben McCulloch of the Texas Rangers to confirm the existence of this force and to bring him accurate information about its size and composition. McCulloch located Santa Anna just south of La Encarnación, and, slipping past Mexican sentries under cover of night, he climbed a hill in the midst of the enemy camp from where, next morning, he enjoyed a sweeping view of the enemy encampment. Having returned through the lines the next night, the ranger reported to Taylor early in the morning of the twenty-first of February, giving him a complete report on the approaching army.

But even as McCulloch was reporting to his commander, Santa Anna began his advance. Sending a large cavalry detachment off to the right with instructions to reach the American rear, he moved directly against Agua Nueva with his main body. As reports of this movement arrived, Taylor, knowing his position to be indefensible, gave the order to fall back. At noon on the twenty-first, leaving only a token force to guard supplies which could not be moved, the American army began its retreat to a defensive position near Buena Vista Ranch which had earlier been decided upon. Leaving Wool in command at this point, Taylor hurried on to Saltillo to supervise personally the preparation of defenses at this all-important base.

Santa Anna's advance pressed rapidly forward. The small American detachment left to guard the precious supplies were forced to retreat but not before setting fire to the stores to prevent their falling into Mexican hands. Convinced now that the entire American army was retreating in disorder, Santa Anna ordered a forced march in order to overtake and destroy the demoralized enemy. Pursuit was continued until dark and was resumed early next morning. With no little surprise, then, did the Mexicans, expecting to find the enemy in full flight, discover them drawn up in battle array to defend their selected position.

This position had been chosen because it offered the greatest defensive possibilities for Taylor's inferior numbers. Its strength was so clearly apparent that Santa Anna cautiously paused to survey his intrenched enemy before ordering an assault. What he saw was enough to confirm his worst fears. The key to the American position was the Narrows, or La Angostura, a barely passable, point on the road from San Luis Potosí to Saltillo. On the western side of the road, a network of eroded gullies and ditches made attack from that direction impossible; on the east, several long spurs from the nearby mountain range stretched down nearly to the edge of the road. Wool, placing his artillery so as to command the road, formed his battle line, composed of some forty-seven hundred men, from the Narrows eastward along the dominant spur toward the foot of the mountains.

After reconnoitering the American position, Santa Anna clearly saw that only one course of action was left open to him. It was obviously impossible to attack on the enemy right because of the terrain; it would be foolhardy to move against the center, with American artillery in so commanding a position; therefore, any assault must necessarily be made against the left flank. But before launching any attack, the confident Santa Anna gave his opponent one last opportunity to surrender. Under a flag of truce he sent Taylor, who had now returned from Saltillo, a letter pointing out to him the hopelessness of his situation and informing him that his tiny army, surrounded now by twenty thousand troops, would inevitably be cut to pieces. Expressing a desire to save Taylor from such a "catastrophe," Santa Anna gave him one hour in which to surrender and closed his message with the assurance that the vanquished would be treated with the "consideration belonging to the Mexican character." Taylor, with commendable confidence in his small army, unhesitatingly replied in the negative. Upon receipt of this answer, Santa Anna began to make serious preparation for an attack.

The fighting on the twenty-second was inconclusive. About three o'clock in the afternoon, the Mexicans struck the American left wing and began a struggle which lasted in that quarter until nightfall without producing any decisive results. That night, after the firing had ceased, Taylor again returned to Saltillo to bolster defenses there while his troops literally slept on their guns, shivering in the cold, drizzling rain which began to fall.

The main fighting in the Battle of Buena Vista took place

on February 23. Shortly after daybreak, mass was celebrated by the Mexican army while the Americans, from their intrenched position, watched with awe this splendid ritual. When the service was over, Santa Anna unleashed a savage attack on the American left which sent the defenders in that quarter reeling backward. Before Taylor had even returned to the battlefield from Saltillo, his left wing was smashed and his troops from that sector of the line were being hurled back in confusion toward the ranch house at Buena Vista. By nine o'clock in the morning, Taylor's army was threatened with disaster, for the path to their rear had been opened on the left flank, which meant that the enemy might either wheel and fall upon the troops at the Narrows or move directly against Saltillo or both. At this critical juncture, while Santa Anna was preparing to deliver the final blow, Taylor hurried upon the scene accompanied by reinforcements from Saltillo. Seeing at once the seriousness of the situation, he ordered the Mississippians to advance on the double. Holding their fire until they had dashed well within range, these troops suddenly opened a murderous and devastating fire which broke the Mexican charge and forced them to fall back. So passed the morning with the Mexican attack at first succeeding brilliantly in threatening to envelop the defensive line—only to suffer, at the moment of triumph, a reverse from Taylor's reinforcements in a charge that probably saved the day for the Americans.

Shortly after noon, Santa Anna ordered another large-scale attack on the American left, this time with the object of gaining possession of the Saltillo Road in the rear of the line. This maneuver led to some of the bloodiest fighting of the day. After allowing the Mexicans to advance into the open end of a triangular defensive position, the Americans opened a withering fire. The oncoming Mexicans, as though deliberately seeking to aid their own destruction, stopped dead still in the midst of this biting fire, and the Americans rushed upon them using knife and bayonet at close range. A violent rainstorm did nothing to halt the ferocious combat which continued to rage until the Mexicans slowly retreated. By early afternoon, Taylor's men had reoccupied most of the ground they had lost during the morning and had succeeded in removing the grave threat to their rear.

More bitter fighting was yet to come. About four in the afternoon, Taylor attempted to seize the initiative and ordered a charge in which three of his regiments were decimated. This abortive maneuver was followed by one last massive Mexican attack, launched this time directly against the center of the American line. At first, the defenders were pushed back by the pressure of sheer numbers, but, as their massed artillery began to tear gaping holes in the advancing columns, Santa Anna recalled his men. Within an hour, the fighting had ended; a unofficial truce, dictated by exhaustion, followed. Tactically, it was a drawn battle; the American forces were badly battered, to be sure, but they had not been dislodged from the position they had taken. The arrival of reinforcements from the garrison at Rinconada that night made it possible for Taylor to face the enemy next morning with a force roughly equal to the one with which he had begun that bloody day's fighting.

During the night, Santa Anna, whose earlier confidence in victory was now badly shaken, grew increasingly discouraged over the condition of his own troops. As he viewed the situation, his choice was either to risk another battle next morning or to retreat with his forces intact and claim success on the basis of those visible symbols of victory, flags and guns, which he had captured early in the battle. The latter alternative was infinitely more inviting, and Santa Anna, preferring a bird in the hand, ordered that the picket fires be kept burning to deceive the enemy while he stealthily began to pull out his main army during the night of the twenty-third. Next morning, when the benumbed American soldiers discovered that the enemy had withdrawn, their exultation knew no bounds; even the usually reticent commander embraced Wool in an impetuous hug.

Later in the day, Taylor sent a messenger to Santa Anna suggesting an exchange of prisoners and return of the wounded, and at the same time expressing a hope for peace. The Mexican leader agreed to the exchange, stated his inability to carry off his wounded, and emphatically refused to discuss the issue of peace while enemy troops remained on Mexican soil. With that parting shot, the self-styled "Napoleon of the West" set out for San Luis Potosí, a march which in its effect upon his dwindling army was somewhat reminiscent of the earlier and more disastrous retreat of his namesake from Moscow.

With the Battle of Buena Vista, the campaign in northern Mexico came to an end. From that time on, there were no major offensives in that area, and during the remainder of the war the army there remained wholly on the defensive, merely holding the line already established.

In the ten months since Thornton's capture, the American army had enjoyed a continuing series of almost incredible successes. They had defeated a Mexican army three times their size at Palo Alto and Resaca de la Palma. They had occupied Matamoros, Reynosa, Camargo, and other strategic points in the area. They had wrested the prize city of Monterrey from its defenders. They had occupied Saltillo and taken a position beyond that city where an immensely superior Mexican army had been fought to a standstill and then forced to retreat.

The navy, in supporting the northern campaign, enjoyed no comparable victories since their primary task was simply to enforce the blockade. Nasty weather, uncharted reefs, and tricky currents caused a number of shipwrecks and did nothing to lessen the embarrassment resulting from two bootless attempts to capture Alvarado, a port not far from Veracruz.

Among the personalities involved, General Zachary Taylor profited more than any other individual from these operations. His prestige and popularity skyrocketed as the campaign progressed. When the American public set about fashioning the Father-Protector image that it reserves for its successful military heroes, it was inevitable that they should also begin to think and talk of him in political terms. The General's political star began to rise after the victories of Palo Alto and Resaca de la Palma, gained momentum after his conquest of Monterrey, and reached its zenith after his dramatic defense at Buena Vista.

Admittedly, the campaign in northern Mexico was not decisive in the sense that it brought the Mexican nation to its knees. It did not bring the war to an end for the simple reason that it was fought too far away from the Mexican heartland. It did not strike at the enemy's vital center. But it did provide a badly needed boost to the morale of the American army and public. It did settle with finality the question of this country's ability to maintain its boundary along the Rio Grande line. And it did manufacture the next President of the United States.

III

Thrust to the Pacific

While General Zachary Taylor was vigorously prosecuting the war in northern Mexico, other events, equally important though less highly publicized, were taking place beyond the western boundary of the United States. Long before the beginning of hostilities between the two countries, the United States had displayed what seemed to many Mexicans a disproportionate interest in the provinces of New Mexico and California. The abortive Texan Santa Fe expedition and Commodore Jones's presumptuous seizure of Monterey Bay were merely the cruder expressions of a deep-seated American desire to acquire these two provinces from Mexico.

Both provinces, to be sure, were tempting targets. Although New Mexico, with its prized caravan trade centered in Santa Fe, refrained from displaying any compelling desire to be annexed, it offered every promise of easy conquest. And even though the governor, Manuel Armijo, spoke bravely of erecting fortifications and calling up troops to defend the area, no one really expected serious military opposition from that quarter. There was a general feeling that a relatively small, irregular force could easily overrun New Mexico. The situation in California was only slightly different, for by the mid-1840's it was virtually a derelict on the international scene. Practically abandoned by the Mexican government, the small scattered population was ridden with disaffection and unrest. An independence movement was only one of several flourishing intrigues. Although several powers were interested in acquiring the province, there was some justification for the feeling prevalent in the United States that California would eventually come into the Union without military conquest but rather as a result of the same sort of peaceful infiltration that had secured Texas. In both these distant provinces the central government had virtually lost all effective control; in both there existed a revolutionary spirit that could easily be exploited; and both were sadly lacking in the means of defending themselves. The absence of effective opposition in New Mexico and the distinct possibility of peaceful acquisition of California were the two most common arguments advanced in support of the popularly held belief that eventual possession of the two areas by the United States was inevitable.

As the two countries drifted toward war, however, more positive plans were laid for the acquisition of these two coveted regions. It is obvious that the administration in Washington, from the first moment that war with Mexico appeared to be a real possibility, meant to seize and occupy them as part of the basic war strategy. As early as 1845, the naval force stationed off the California coast was strengthened, and Commodore J. D. Sloat, senior officer present afloat, was issued specific instructions to seize San Francisco and other important points should war between the United States and Mexico actually break out. In May, 1846, upon receipt in Washington of the news of fighting along the Rio Grande, Sloat's orders were reiterated and enlarged to include the capture of Monterey and the institution of a blockade wherever such action might be deemed necessary. Additional vessels were ordered to join the flotilla already on station, infantry reinforcements were loaded aboard ships on the East Coast and sent on their way, and the expedition being readied for the invasion of New Mexico was instructed to be prepared to render later assistance in the conquest of California. This force was to march overland to New Mexico, to seize Santa Fe, and garrison the area. As soon as conditions there permitted, a detachment was to move on to California and co-operate with American forces already on the scene.

These basic orders set in motion the various military forces whose primary role was to fight the war on the enemy's periphery. Their task was to seize and occupy coveted Mexican territories far distant from the enemy's heartland. While the American public was avidly reading the more popular stories of fighting along the Rio Grande, less-known but immensely significant western campaigns were being fought on this remote, neglected frontier.

The expedition to capture New Mexico was assigned to the command of Colonel Stephen W. Kearny, an exceedingly able and energetic officer of the regular army. In May, 1846, Kearny received the original orders to prepare for an invasion of that province, and by the end of June he had welded together at Fort Leavenworth some fifteen hundred frontiersmen into what was officially termed the "Army of the West." On the twenty-seventh of that month he began his advance along the Santa Fe Trail, and, averaging a hundred miles a week for five weeks, he arrived at Bent's Fort on the Arkansas early in August. After a short delay to rest his weary troops and to await the reinforcements following him, Kearny resumed his march to the southwest.

On the fourteenth of August, he made his first contact with the enemy. An envoy from Armijo, under a flag of truce, approached him with the truculent message that the Governor had every intention of offering resistance if the Americans continued their advance. Without giving the slightest consideration to this threat, Kearny moved on, and the following day the village of Las Vegas was taken. On the sixteenth, San Miguel was occupied; the Americans were now closing in on Santa Fe. At this point, word reached the camp of the invaders that Armijo had moved into position at Apache Pass, a strong defensive position on the road leading to Santa Fe, but, in spite of this ominous news, Kearny remained firm in his decision to advance on the capital. As the Americans moved forward on the seventeenth, Armijo suddenly abandoned his position and retreated, allowing the invading army to secure its objective without a struggle. Thus, on the sixteenth of August, while Taylor was encamped at Camargo preparing to advance upon Monterrey, the American flag was raised at Santa Fe as the Army of the West took formal possession of what some of its members now derisively called "mud town." Kearny immediately issued a proclamation absolving the inhabitants of all allegiance to the Mexican government, claiming them as citizens of the United States and, in an effort at conciliation, guaranteed to all the protection of person, property, and religion. After many of the more prominent citizens had come forward to take the oath, the bulk of the population followed suit, and relative quiet descended upon the region. This brought to a successful conclusion the six-week campaign in which fifteen hundred men, after marching more than a thousand miles, had taken undisputed possession of a country with an estimated eighty thousand inhabitants. In spite of the fact that the territory offered strong natural defenses, the conquest had been accomplished without firing a gun.

Kearny now busied himself in a variety of endeavors. Though primarily involved in completing construction of Fort Marcy, he also found time to oversee preparation of a code of laws for the territory and even won some friends on the local scene by the appointment of the well-known Charles Bent as governor. But as the situation in New Mexico stabilized, Kearny grew more impatient to get on with the rest of his assignment—to move on to California and aid in its conquest. The apparent calm and tranquillity in the occupied province and the news that reinforcements were on the way only confirmed Kearny's strong belief that there were more men in New Mexico than were actually needed. In an effort to employ his available manpower more effectively, he laid plans for two separate movements, both to originate from the Santa Fe command. One was an advance toward California which he planned to command personally as soon as his relief, Colonel Sterling Price, arrived in Santa Fe. The second campaign was to be a movement against Chihuahua. Command of this expedition was intrusted to Alexander W. Doniphan, a Missouri lawyer whose personality uniquely fitted him for the assignment.

Kearny, however, did not remain in Santa Fe to see the Chihuahua expedition launched. On the twenty-fifth of September, confident that all was secure in the area, he departed for California even though his relief, Price, was still three days' march away. With three hundred men, Kearny headed westward across the roadless desert wastes and rugged mountain ranges between him and his destination. Two weeks later he unexpectedly encountered the famous scout Kit Carson, who gave him a detailed description of the "complete conquest" of California that had already occurred. Upon receipt of this encouraging news, Kearny sent half his force back to New Mexico, and in company with Carson, who had been persuaded to act as guide, he and the remnant of his command continued their trek to California. Having endured the hardships of a thousand-mile march, this hardy band reached the California boundary early in December only to discover that the Californians had revolted against American occupation forces and had succeeded in dispossessing their recent conquerors. In short, Kearny and his handful of weary troopers had arrived in California at a crucial moment. In place of the cozy garrison duty that had been envisioned since Carson's first glowing account of victory, they were now faced with the prospect of a hard, active campaign.

Meanwhile Doniphan's Chihuahua venture had been readied; by mid-December, 1846, he was making last-minute preparations at Valverde, the starting point for the expedition. On the twelfth of that month, the advance toward El Paso commenced, and, after a harrowing passage through the forbidding Jornada del Muerto, the force arrived on Christmas Day at El Brazito, thirty miles north of El Paso. Here they first encountered the enemy, and after a fruitless parley, the Mexicans charged the Americans, firing harmlessly at long range. Doniphan's men held their fire until the advancing columns were almost upon them. Then, suddenly, they poured two rapid, devastating volleys that broke the charge and drove the Mexicans back in the direction of the city. In this first engagement, Doniphan defeated a force twice his number in the open field without losing a man. Next day, as he marched toward El Paso, a deputation of citizens came to him to surrender the city, which was formally occupied on the twenty-seventh.

Doniphan and his men passed the month of January, 1847, in El Paso, but in early February the march to Chihuahua was resumed. The road to the south cut through an arid region where the scarcity of water and food was aggravated by an abundance of insects and reptiles. But in spite of all hardships the advance continued, and finally, on the twenty-seventh of February, Doniphan and his men reached the Sacramento River some fifteen miles from Chihuahua. Here they discovered the Mexicans settled into positions of undeniable strength. Using nature as their ally, they had so situated their forces as to make a frontal assault unavoidable, and the American commander, surveying their position, ordered the attack. Under the protection of the banks of a dried-up riverbed, Doniphan moved his troops off to the right and unexpectedly struck what appeared to be the weakest point in the enemy's defenses, their left flank. The fighting was furious for a while, but by five o'clock that afternoon it was all over: the Mexicans had been driven from their position and the road to Chihuahua now lay open. On March 2, without further opposition, the city was occupied by American troops.

The remainder of the Doniphan story is brief. In late April he was ordered by the War Department to join Taylor's command, and, marching another six hundred miles through the heart of the enemy's country without so much as a serious challenge, he reported in late May to his superior officer's headquarters in Monterrey. From there, he and his tireless frontiersmen were shipped home, reaching New Orleans in mid-June, and were finally mustered out of the service early in July in St. Louis. All in all, theirs had been a full year. They had marched several thousand miles, participated in the conquest of New Mexico, captured Chihuahua, and marched almost at will through the enemy's country defeating every force thrown against them. Yet in spite of these splendid achievements, the march of "Doniphan's Thousand" had little real effect on the outcome of the war, for the government soon abandoned any idea of holding Chihuahua. Nevertheless, their exploits furnished an impressive example of just how much could be accomplished, in spite of awesome obstacles, by a relatively small group of determined men without specific orders, uniforms, pay, or discipline.

Back in New Mexico, in the meantime, the calm that had descended following the American occupation continued. On September 28, three days after Kearny's departure for California, Colonel Sterling Price arrived in Santa Fe and assumed the duties of military commander of the area. For the following two and a half months the placidity of life in the province continued to belie the seething unrest and resentment of the inhabitants. In the middle of December, however, the true state of affairs was exposed by the unsettling discovery of a carefully laid plot among the Mexicans to rise in unison and kill all Americans in the territory. The leaders of the projected uprising fled as soon as their plot was discovered. Though Price failed to capture any of the ringleaders, he abruptly inaugurated a more repressive occupation policy. This pressure only worsened an already bad situation, for less than a month after the new policies were initiated, open rebellion broke out in the province.

Thrust to the Pacific

As the result of a carefully detailed and well-executed plan, Governor Bent and several other officials of the government were assassinated and barbarously mutilated in mid-January, 1847. Price, as military commander of the area, took immediate steps to crush the rebellion and by January 23 had organized a force which he felt confident was sufficient to restore order. Then in a whirlwind two-week campaign, Price decisively stamped out all resistance by smashing the rebels at Taos, focal point of their operations. So complete was his victory that quiet was restored on more than a temporary basis: New Mexico, for the rest of the war, remained in American hands without serious challenge from within or without.

The conquest of California, eventually accomplished through joint army-navy action, was by far the most important of the western campaigns. United States interest in that province had long been known, and our future intentions were unmistakably reflected not only in the unequivocal orders issued to the American naval commander in Pacific waters but also by the "scientific" expedition that was sent into that general area under the command of an enigmatic young officer of the regular army, Captain John C. Frémont. These combined land and naval forces were to play the dominant role in seizing California when war actually broke out between the United States and Mexico.

The Frémont expedition, ostensibly an exploring trip to the Pacific Coast sponsored by the federal government, set out in the fall of 1845 and by January of 1846, months before fighting began on the Rio Grande, had arrived in northern California. Presumably to give his men some respite from the cold weather and to allow them to rest while he recruited more men for his command, Frémont moved in the direction of southern California, where, upon receiving permission from the authorities, he pitched camp. His choice of a campsite proved unwise, however; its proximity to Monterey gave rise to fears and misgivings on the part of local officials who early in March peremptorily ordered the captain and his party out of the country. Frémont at first refused to move, but within a week, yielding to the pressure of necessity, he departed for the north. Six weeks later, while in the vicinity of the Oregon boundary, Frémont was overtaken by a special messenger from Washington, bringing him the latest reports from the government. Abruptly reversing his course, the young captain and his followers moved southward once again, this time to play an active role in the acquisition of California.

During June and July, Frémont's force remained in and around Sonoma, where they fought several skirmishes and were instrumental in bringing about the farcical "Bear Flag Revolt." On July 4, the "independence" of California was unabashedly proclaimed. The troubles that might have resulted from the embarrassing lack of local support of this coup were avoided, because within only a few days word arrived confirming the rumors of war between the United States and Mexico. This announcement led immediately to the lowering of the Bear Flag and to its replacement by the Stars and Stripes. Having contributed his bit to the advancement of United States interests in that area, Frémont now departed for Monterey to co-operate with other American forces on the scene in the further conquest of California.

The navy, in the meantime, had been engaged in carrying out the government's earlier orders concerning California. On July 7, upon receipt of reliable news of the fighting at Palo

Alto and the Resaca de la Palma, Commodore Sloat, after a period of indecision, probably brought on as much by the embarrassment of the Catesby Jones fiasco of 1842 as by his own ill health, finally decided to act. On that same day, Monterey was captured and the American flag was immediately hoisted over the town. Three days later, the San Francisco area was occupied by a naval force and with these major coastal points secured, attention was turned to the seizure of enemy strong points in the interior.

At this point, Commodore Robert F. Stockton arrived with orders to relieve Sloat; in mid-July the change of command was completed and the ailing Sloat headed for home. The new commander had hardly assumed his duties, however, before his first problem arose. On the nineteenth of July, Frémont arrived in Monterey; his appearance revived the thorny question of command prerogatives which has been so persistent a theme in American military affairs whenever the sister services have found it necessary to act in concert. As the result of a conference between the captain and the commodore, a *modus vivendi* was reached: Stockton, as senior officer, retained the top command, but the California Battalion, the irregular field force now organized, was intrusted to the tactical command of Frémont.

By the latter part of July, the commodore was ready to move against Los Angeles, strongest enemy garrison in southern California. On the twenty-fourth of July, he dispatched Frémont and his men by water to San Diego, from where they were to move overland against the city. Another force, under Stockton's personal command, moved to San Pedro, which was to be the base for a second movement against the citadel. While waiting for Frémont to move up from San Diego, the commodore decided to risk an advance against the enemy, who, to his surprise and gratitude fled their position. Without opposition Stockton occupied Los Angeles on August 13 and shortly thereafter issued a proclamation naming himself governor of the territory and offering the usual guarantees of protection to the inhabitants. Thus, while General Taylor was still at Camargo, the occupation of California was accomplished practically without firing a gun. In fact, the situation seemed so well in hand that Stockton confidently reported to Washington that all was secure. He now toyed with the idea of turning the California theater of operations over to Frémont, so that he might devote his full attention to naval operations against Mexican seaports in Lower California. Riding high on this wave of optimism, Stockton left a small garrison in Los Angeles and set out in early September for San Francisco. Meanwhile, the equally confident Frémont had moved northward in search of more recruits. Neither Stockton nor Frémont anticipated the rude shock immediately in store for them.

Near the end of September, Stockton received at San Francisco the startling news that the Californians had revolted, that all southern California was in arms, and that his small garrison in Los Angeles was sorely besieged. What he could not know was that the United States garrison had already been forced to surrender after a week-long defense against overwhelming numbers. Stockton sent a hurried order to Frémont, who was still on recruiting duty in northern California, to return by forced marches. While awaiting his arrival, the commodore was busy at San Francisco making plans for another expedition against Los Angeles.

By the second week in October, Frémont had returned. Stockton, now ready to move, determined to employ again the

plan that had proved successful in the earlier operation: Frémont was to proceed by way of San Diego while Stockton
moved off to San Pedro. Poor liaison, however, played havoc
with the commodore's plan, for Frémont, presumably in order
to procure horses for his command, violated his instructions
and went ashore at Monterey instead of proceeding to San
Diego. Stockton, with only a token force at San Pedro, was in
no position to attack. After waiting vainly for Frémont's arrival, he moved down to San Diego in November.

As the end of the year approached, then, the outlook for
American forces in California was dismal. Enemy troops were
in possession of most of the towns in the interior and were
actively threatening coastal positions; Stockton remained sty-
mied at San Diego without sufficient strength to advance;
Frémont was wandering somewhere in the hinterland; and
Kearny's bedraggled force coming overland from New Mexico
had only recently reached the California border. Stockton
realized the necessity of concentrating at least some elements
of his scattered command as a prerequisite to any offensive
action, and, since he had no reliable information on the where-
abouts of Frémont, he sent a message to Kearny telling him of
the desperate situation in California and urging him to hasten
to San Diego. The message reached Kearny on December 5,
and, characteristically, he prepared to move forward immediately. This last leg of his long journey was to prove the most
difficult, however, for the same messenger from Stockton
brought the even more discouraging news that a strong enemy
force lay intrenched a few miles up the road.

In spite of this ominous development, Kearny, keenly aware
of Stockton's plight, moved forward on the morning of December 6. In no time at all, he encountered the enemy and fought

the short, bloody Battle of San Pasqual. Though the Californians were driven from their positions, the cost to the Americans was high: nearly a third of the small command was killed, and Kearny himself was wounded. So critical was their condition that a messenger was sent to San Diego, thirty miles away, with an urgent plea for help. Next day, Kearny moved his battered troops into a defensive position along the banks of the San Bernardo River, where he intended to await the arrival of a relief expedition from Stockton. There he remained unmolested on December 8 and 9 but on the tenth the enemy struck. Their attempt to demoralize the defenders by stampeding a herd of horses through the camp failed. The Americans held with tenacity, then pushed the attackers back. That night the anxiously awaited reinforcements arrived, and on the following day the march was resumed. On the twelfth of December, Kearny and his hundred exhausted troopers finally reached their destination.

When Kearny's fatigued command had rested in San Diego, Stockton once again moved against Los Angeles. In spite of Frémont's absence, the commodore now had a motley force of some five hundred soldiers, sailors, marines, and irregulars, as well as half a dozen pieces of artillery. With this nondescript command, he moved out of San Diego on December 29 and headed toward his objective. His advance was virtually unimpeded until he arrived in the vicinity of the city. On the eighth of January he encountered the enemy drawn up on the opposite bank of the San Gabriel River, their artillery commanding the ford from a nearby bluff. Stockton refused to be intimidated by these impressive defenses, and his troops, passing down the ranks the battle cry "New Orleans," in memory of Andrew Jackson's smashing defeat of the British on that same date thirty-two years earlier, attacked with such vigor that the enemy soon withdrew. Next day, as the advance on Los Angeles continued, the antagonists fought yet another battle and once again the defenders failed to halt the American advance. As preparations for a general assault were being completed on the morning of the tenth, a delegation from the city came out under a flag of truce with the news that Los Angeles had been evacuated and offered to surrender the city to the invaders. Later that same day, Stockton's men entered Los Angeles and, after quelling a series of riots and disorders, firmly resumed American occupation of the city.

While these events were taking place in the south, the elusive Frémont had not remained idle. When enough additional men had been recruited in northern and central California to bring his force up to nearly four hundred, he moved toward the south in late November. On the twelfth of January, two days after Stockton had taken possession of Los Angeles, Frémont arrived outside the city, where, having made contact with the enemy's field forces, he independently negotiated the Treaty of Cahuenga. Since Frémont signed this treaty as "military commander" and granted to the enemy terms which Stockton had earlier refused them, there is no escaping the fact that the presumptuous captain had coolly gone over the heads of both the commodore and the brigadier general who had done the lion's share of the fighting. Incredible though it may seem, Stockton, apparently anxious to get on with naval pursuits, approved Frémont's treaty after a conference between the two men on January 13.

Thus, some six weeks before Taylor's battle at Buena Vista and over two months before Scott's landing at Veracruz, the rich prize of California had fallen to the Americans. With the reoccupation of Los Angeles, all organized resistance in the area ceased. There was still an occasional local riot or other minor disorder, but the only significant fighting yet to occur in that province was between American officers, who, in defeating the enemy had unwittingly loosened the tenuous bonds that made their temporary co-operation possible.

IV

To the City of Mexico

Even though the war in northern Mexico had been spectacularly successful for United States forces, it soon became apparent that this would not be the decisive theater of operations. The disastrous sequence of military reverses suffered by Mexico and the subsequent occupation of a large portion of her northernmost provinces failed to produce the desired results; in spite of these setbacks, Mexico showed no disposition to end the war. The realization in Washington that the war in the north had been ineffective led to the formulation of a new strategy. Since war on the periphery had failed to produce decisive results, the war would now be carried to the Mexican heartland. There were two possible ways this might be accomplished. One was for Taylor to move overland from his position in northern Mexico to San Luis Potosí and Mexico City; but this proposal was rejected because of the vastness of the intervening desert and the tremendous distances involved. An alternative to the overland approach was to transport an army by water to a Mexican coastal port from which an advance upon the capital might be made. This was the plan finally adopted. As early as October, 1846, President Polk had decided upon a movement against Mexico City by way of the Gulf port of Veracruz, a route following the path of Cortez and his *conquistadores*.

ROUTE FROM VERACRUZ TO MEXICO CITY

With a plan of campaign settled, the President needed to find a suitable commander to execute it. Polk would gladly have bypassed both Taylor and Scott. But he finally yielded, though gracelessly and with misgivings, to the combined dictates of propriety and necessity, and through the simple process of elimination gave the post to General Scott. On November 23, Secretary of War Marcy issued formal instructions to that officer, and, in spite of their vagueness and ambiguity, Scott began immediately to requisition supplies and make other preparations for the campaign. Because of the shortage of available manpower, Scott was forced to notify Taylor that a number of troops would have to be withdrawn from the northern theater of war in order to carry out the invasion which the administration now assigned highest priority. Shortly thereafter, the General left Washington and went in person to northern Mexico, where he spent the early part of the new year gathering his forces. Ordering Taylor to remain on the defensive, Scott moved on to Lobos Island, where he arrived on the twenty-first of February. This site, some seven miles off the Mexican coast just below Tampico, had been selected by the commander as the staging area for the expedition because its protected harbor was sufficiently large to accommodate the assembled fleet. In the week following, Scott was busy reorganizing his force, which now totaled nearly ten thousand men, working out a detailed plan of debarkation and making countless last-minute adjustments and preparations.

On March 2, 1847, the fleet sailed from its Lobos Island anchorage and after a rough, stormy four-day passage reassembled off Antón Lizardo, the previously agreed upon rendezvous twelve miles south of Veracruz. After two additional days of reconnoitering, Scott began the largest amphibious assault that had ever been attempted by an American force. On March 9 a landing was made on the beach three miles southeast of Veracruz opposite Sacraficios Island, a site selected earlier by the ranking naval officer, Commodore P. S. P. Conner, and approved by Scott. Without any accurate knowledge of the kind or amount of opposition that would be offered by the Mexicans, many of whom could be seen riding among the dunes on the beach, the assault troops were ordered from their transports. They crowded into the surf boats that had been specifically constructed for this operation and, under a protective barrage of naval gunfire, were towed toward the shore in formation. Upon reaching a point within a hundred yards of the beach, the men leaped into the surf and holding their guns over their heads waded ashore behind their division commander, the short-tempered former commandant of cadets at West Point, General William Jenkins Worth, "the Murat of the American Army." The Mexicans, in failing to offer any real opposition to the landing, made the first in a long line of mistakes that aided the Americans in their conquest. In any amphibious assault, the crucial period lies between the time the troops have left their transports and the time they have securely established a beachhead. In this particular landing, the normal vulnerability of the American force was greatly increased by the crowding of the advancing surf boats and the confusion on the beach. Thanks primarily to Mexican negligence, the entire force was landed without serious interference; by nightfall on March 9, ten thousand United States soldiers were on the beach below Veracruz.

The ensuing week was spent in firmly establishing the beachhead and in formulating a specific tactical plan for the seizure of Veracruz. While reserves of stores and supplies were being built up on the beach, Scott wrestled with the problem of how best to take the walled city before him. Veracruz, long a favorite port of entry for invaders, possessed strong fortifications manned by four thousand troops. In the harbor, about half a mile from the town, stood the seemingly impregnable fortress of San Juan de Ulúa, garrisoned by an additional twelve hundred men. Fully as forbidding as either of these was the menace of yellow fever, which continued to plague Scott's troops as long as they remained in the lowlands along the coast. After a careful weighing of all these considerations, Scott, in the interest of saving American lives, decided to besiege the city, to bypass the rugged fortress in the harbor and force the city to surrender by cutting it off from the rear. While preparations for the siege were being pushed, the desire of Scott's men for comparable honors was sharpened by the news of Taylor's victory at Buena Vista.

By the sixteenth of March, the investment of Veracruz was completed. The city was now sealed off from the rear by American forces arranged in an arc-shaped line some seven miles long. This line, begun in the south by Worth's regulars, extended across the center by the volunteers under the command of Major General Robert Patterson and anchored at the northern end by the division of the profane "Bengal Tiger," David Twiggs. In spite of bad weather that plagued operations, trenches were dug, siege batteries were constructed, the water supply into Veracruz was closed off, rail transportation and communications were severed, and all roads leading into the city were closed. By March 22 the fortress city was so closely surrounded that it was now virtually impossible for the Mexicans either to escape or to receive help. Certain that the city could be pounded into submission, Scott, shortly after noon on that day, formally demanded its surrender, and, when the defenders, still confident of their ability to hold off the Americans, refused to accede to his terms, he began the bombardment of Veracruz.

For forty-eight hours this relentless battering continued. Within the city, buildings were smashed by shells or gutted by fire, gaping holes were torn in the streets, and each successive explosion increased the toll of dead and wounded. In desperation the foreign consuls approached Scott's headquarters on the evening of the twenty-fourth, seeking a truce in order to allow women, children, and neutrals to evacuate the beleaguered city. The American commander, counting on such internal pressure to help bring about the city's surrender, refused their request, and, reminding them of his earlier warning to clear the area, he repeated his statement that there could be no truce without surrender. He added, pointedly, that anyone, soldier or non-combatant, who attempted to leave the city would be fired upon.

Next morning, the bombardment was intensified. Despair now permeated the helpless city. On March 26 negotiations for its surrender were begun, and on the following day an agreement was reached by the contracting parties. Under its terms, the garrison was allowed to march out with the honors of war, the sick and wounded were granted sanctuary within the city, Mexican troops were paroled, and, while all public property in Veracruz was to be confiscated, private property was to be scrupulously respected.

At noon on March 29, 1847, the Mexicans stacked their arms; shortly thereafter, United States forces marched in and raised the American flag over the City of the True Cross. General Scott, from his new headquarters in the governor's palace, created the Military Department of Veracruz and appointed General Worth as military governor. Rations were distributed, efforts were made to clean up the area to forestall an outbreak of yellow fever, martial law was declared in an attempt to restore order, and in a short time the city returned to everyday activity.

Once again the Mexicans had surrendered a strongly fortified city after a trifling defense. At the time of surrender the garrison still had food, water, and ammunition, and the fortress of San Juan de Ulúa was virtually untouched. So feeble, in fact, was Mexican resistance that the landing, siege, and conquest were accomplished with less than one hundred American casualties! With the occupation of Veracruz, the invaders had now established a base upon Mexican soil from which United States naval forces could mount expeditions to capture Alvarado and Tuxpan and from which General Scott could now begin his projected march overland to Mexico City.

General Santa Anna in the meantime had not remained idle. After the Battle of Buena Vista he returned to San Luis Potosí and, while resting his weary command, received word of a new revolt against the government. On March 14, at the time Scott was completing his line of investment around Veracruz, Santa Anna issued one of his many wartime proclamations to the Mexican people promising that he would not only put an end to domestic turmoil but also defeat the new invading force. Then, sending part of his forces in haste toward Veracruz, Santa Anna, accompanied by the remainder of his army, set out for Mexico City. Awaiting him on his arrival a week later were the manifold and perplexing problems of restoring order in the city. He had to deal with the strong political opposition that had congealed, and he needed to raise money and manpower to meet the enemy threat from the coast. With almost unbelievable swiftness he re-established order and pacified or suppressed his opposition. He was already engrossed in raising troops when the news of the fall of Veracruz reached the capital. Three days later, the indefatigable Santa Anna was en route to the coast. On April 5, he established his headquarters at Encero, where he put the finishing touches on his plan to meet the advancing enemy at the mountain pass of Cerro Gordo. Thus, within a month after the fighting at Buena Vista, the energetic Mexican commander had traveled over a thousand miles, stabilized the government, throttled his political opponents, replenished the treasury, and reorganized the army.

Now he readied his forces to meet the Americans along the road to Mexico City.

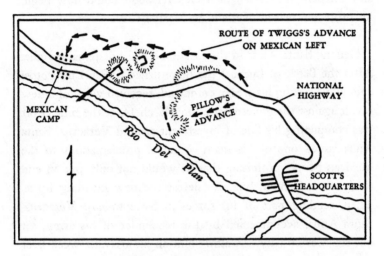

BATTLE OF CERRO GORDO

With his base securely established at Veracruz, General Scott, spurred on by his fear of a yellow fever epidemic in the lowlands, made final preparations for an advance. On April 8, Twiggs's division moved out up the National Highway, followed the next day by Patterson's command. Their immediate destination was Jalapa, a town along the route to Mexico City situated high enough to be free of attack from the dreaded yellow fever. By April 12 the American advance reached the village of Plan del Río, just below the pass at Cerro Gordo. Here Twiggs halted when he encountered Mexican fire and waited for Patterson to move up. Patterson, as senior officer, suspended operations to await the arrival of General Scott. The commanding general rejoined his army on the fourteenth and immediately made a detailed study of the Mexican position. What he saw offered little encouragement, for Santa Anna had skilfully combined his forces with those of nature to create a formidable position. The Mexican defensive line was approximately two miles long stretching from the river on their right, across the National Highway to two hills on their left, Telegraph Hill and La Atalaya. Convinced that the American army, encumbered with artillery and wagon train, could only advance by the highway, the wily Mexican had concentrated his firepower at this point. To the right of the road he had placed batteries on each of the three spurs commanding the route and had moved thirty-five hundred of his best troops into position there. To the left of the road, he had constructed a breastwork atop Telegraph Hill and a lesser work on La Atalaya. His reserves were meanwhile held in readiness at the main camp in the rear of his line.

On the basis of reconnaissance reports, Scott decided that no attack on the Mexican right was feasible because of the river and the high bluffs in that direction. Nor could he hope for success by means of a frontal assault; to march up the highway into Santa Anna's well-laid trap would have been suicidal. His only hope, therefore, was to attack the enemy's left, and, in order to exploit any possibility of a flanking movement in that direction, Scott sent his engineers to give the terrain a minute examination. As a consequence of their search, a path leading off to the Mexican left was discovered, and working parties were immediatley sent out to remove rocks and clear underbrush so that the route would be practicable for moving artillery. Scott's plan of attack now matured: he would mount a deceptive attack on the Mexican right wing while moving his main body of troops to the flank and rear of the Mexican left wing. By Friday, April 16, the bypass route was finally cleared, and, with the arrival of Worth's division, Scott now had approximately eight thousand effective men with which to attempt to drive the enemy from their entrenched position.

In the early morning hours of the seventeenth, Twiggs's division moved off toward the Mexican left with orders to seize La Atalaya on the extreme left of the Mexican line. Santa Anna hastily reinforced his garrison there but was unable to hold it against the American attack. This was the only significant action on that day since both commanders now concentrated on strengthening their forces; Scott sent reinforcements to Twiggs while Santa Anna feverishly shifted forces to meet the charge he now felt certain would be made against Telegraph Hill.

Early Sunday morning Scott opened with his artillery. He then launched a deceptive attack against the Mexican right by troops under the command of Gideon J. Pillow (general by the grace of his former law partner James K. Polk), who made a series of amateurish mistakes that actually nullified his threat. Heavier fighting, meanwhile, developed on the Mexican left. At seven o'clock the order to attack Telegraph Hill was given, and the storming party swept down La Atalaya, across the valley, and up the slope into the galling fire of the defenders. When the summit was gained, the Americans drove the Mexicans from their position after a short but deadly struggle. In the meantime, another American force had moved without detection around the Mexican left flank and at this crucial point emerged in rear of the enemy causing complete confusion in the Mexican encampment. Almost immediately, the Mexicans began a disorganized flight, Santa Anna himself barely escaping capture. By ten o'clock Sunday morning, the battle of

To the City of Mexico

Cerro Gordo was over except for some extracurricular harassment of demoralized Mexicans fleeing toward Jalapa and Puebla. The forbidding mountain pass was now in American hands after a short but decisive fray that netted over three thousand prisoners, large quantities of ammunition, stores, and provisions and—particularly pleasing to the jubilant victors— Santa Anna's personal effects. Next day, having lost less than five hundred men, Scott's army moved on to Jalapa.

Scarcely had the Americanization of that city begun before Scott ordered Worth in pursuit of the retreating Mexicans with orders to capture the city of Perote. As Worth approached the stronghold, the Mexicans evacuated their defensive positions without offering battle, and on April 22, Worth and his men marched into the town, delighted to discover a large store of guns and ammunition left by the recent occupants. At Perote, Worth halted to await further orders from General Scott, who in the meantime remained at Jalapa gathering information, formulating plans, securing provisions, and attempting to persuade his twelve-month volunteers, whose enlistments were now nearly up, to remain in service. Bounty offers proved as unavailing as Scott's personal entreaties to these men, many of whom were veterans of Monterrey and all of whom had seen action at Veracruz and Cerro Gordo. They had freely volunteered, had served their agreed time, and now were ready to be as freely mustered out. They felt, and readily expressed their feeling, that their duty had been done and that others should step forward and make an equal contribution to the cause. Since their enlistments were to expire in six weeks, Scott decided to release them at once. During the first week in May, Patterson led his volunteers back down the road they had so recently traveled, leaving Scott deep within enemy territory with a force of no more than seven thousand soldiers.

On May 6, Worth received orders to advance to Puebla and within a week was on the outskirts of that city. Santa Anna made a halfhearted sortie against him, but, after being repulsed, he evacuated without further contest the second city of Mexico. On the fifteenth of May, Worth's four thousand troops ceremoniously took possession of this city of eighty thousand inhabitants. Before the end of the month, Scott's headquarters were moved to Puebla.

The ten dismal weeks spent at Puebla in the summer of 1847 were a trying period for Scott's little army. The morale of the men, living precariously in the midst of a hostile populace, riddled with dysentery, fatigued by too many hours on the drill field, and annoyed by too few visits from the paymaster, fell to an all time low. Fear of a general uprising of the inhabitants led Scott to call up his troops from Jalapa and Perote, but even this concentration did not provide him with sufficient strength for a forward movement. During July and August the army held on somehow, and, as badly needed reinforcements arrived from Veracruz, Scott began rebuilding his army and welding it into an effective striking force. By early August, this reorganization was completed. His fourteen thousand men were grouped into four divisions; the first was commanded by Worth, the second by Twiggs, the third by Pillow, now a major general, and the fourth by John A. Quitman, the Mississippi hotspur who held the rank of brigadier general of volunteers.

On the morning of August 7, the army set out on the last leg of its journey—destination Mexico City, seventy-five miles to the west. Up through mountain passes ten thousand feet above sea level they trudged until, from the crest, the beautiful valley of Mexico came into view. After a hungry and hurried gaze at this splendid sight, Scott's divisions descended into the valley and assumed their assigned positions. By the twelfth of August, Twiggs was at Ayotla, Quitman at San Isidoro, Worth at Chalco, and Pillow at Chimalpa.

The stage was now set for the last and, as it would soon prove, the bloodiest act of the entire drama. The march overland was now completed and the coveted prize lay almost within their grasp. It was a puny army that presumed to capture a city of two hundred thousand inhabitants, defended by a force three times as large as their own and enjoying the advantage of carefully constructed fortifications. No less an authority than the Duke of Wellington, an avid student of the campaigns being fought on this side of the ocean, grimly prophesied: "Scott is lost—he cannot capture the city and he cannot fall back upon his base."

When the news of the disaster at Cerro Gordo reached Mexico City, a fierce outbreak of anti–Santa Anna sentiment flared up; threats against him were heard on the streets of the capital and charges of cowardice and incompetence were freely levied against him. When he re-entered his nation's capital on May 19, 1847, he found himself once again in desperate straits —abandoned by many of his friends and surrounded by powerful enemies. Ill-fortune was by no means a novelty to Santa Anna; a "time of troubles" is perhaps the most persistent theme in the story of his public life. Adversity seemed to refine his already powerful instinct for survival, and, like a number of history's "strong men" who confidently believed themselves to be Destiny's children, the Mexican leader in time of trial always seemed to have untapped reservoirs of energy to call upon. Acting with dispatch, he bombarded the populace with patriotic proclamations while arresting prominent leaders of the opposition.

When these actions failed to produce their usual result, he changed his tactics. On May 28 he issued an official "resignation" from office, ostensibly to prevent an internal revolution that would have improved the prospects of the advancing enemy. Assuming a favorite pose—that of martyr to his country's interests—Santa Anna ended his letter saying: "I this day terminate forever my public career." Much to the chagrin of the self-sacrificing general, no popular protest was raised. In fact, so obvious was it that his resignation was actually about to be accepted that Santa Anna resorted to another of his many abrupt about-faces. On June 2, before any formal action on his request had been announced, he informed the Mexican Congress that since presenting his resignation he had received new "testimonials of confidence" which made it imperative for him to retain power. He now withdrew his resignation with the expressed desire that "from this moment it shall be held as never having been presented." Having no power to unseat him, the Congress was forced to admit its own debility, and Santa Anna became, in effect, dictator of Mexico.

From this new position of strength he turned assiduously to organizing the defenses of the city. Under the grim slogan "War without pity unto death!" he mobilized available manpower and pushed ahead with the construction of fortifications. By mid-July, he had concentrated in and around Mexico City over twenty-five thousand troops organized into three separate armies: the Army of the East, quartered inside the city; the Army of the South with headquarters just below the city; and the Army of the North which had been ordered down from

To the City of Mexico

San Luis Potosí to Guadalupe Hidalgo, a northern suburb of the capital. Such was the situation within the city as the Americans took up their positions in the Valley of Mexico.

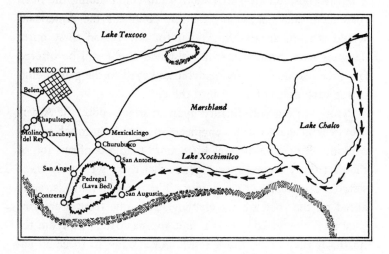

SCOTT'S APPROACH TO MEXICO CITY

The city of Mexico was admirably situated for defense. Surrounded by vast marshlands—remnants of huge lakes—the city could only be entered by one of the numerous causeways connecting it to the surrounding countryside. Thus it was virtually an island approachable by only a limited number of avenues. This natural isolation was a form of defense in itself, but its potential for resistance was greatly increased by well-constructed exterior and interior lines of defense. The outer defenses were erected at all strategic points of entry. The northern approach, by way of Guadalupe Hidalgo, was greatly strengthened; the southern approach, by Mexicalcingo, was guarded by a strong fortification liberally garnished with artillery (south of this point the marsh stretched to the shores of Lakes Chalco and Xochimilco and the mountains beyond). In between these two Santa Anna had erected his most formidable defensive position atop El Peñon, a hill commanding the main road from the east, where he felt confident the Americans would attempt an assault. And if for any reason these outer defenses were breached, stiff resistance might still be offered from the formidable interior defenses keyed to the gates dominating each point of entry into the city.

Before settling with finality upon an attack route, the American general again sent his engineers to make a thorough reconnaissance. Their report was little more than a confirmation of the previously received intelligence that there were only three suitable approaches to the city. They could move straight ahead on the road by which they had come from Veracruz, they might move to the right and approach the city from the north, or they could move south and attempt to force an entrance by the Mexicalcingo route. Each of these possibilities had its drawbacks, however; directly ahead, the impressive position on El Peñon would have to be assaulted; the northern route would involve a forty-mile march around Lake Texcoco and a subsequent attack on the Mexican position at Guadalupe Hidalgo defended by five thousand troops with heavy artillery; the southern route would expose Scott's flank and rear to attack from enemy forces at El Peñon while he was attempting to take Mexicalcingo. Obviously, then, the choice was a difficult one. Scott's engineers believed that the work at El Peñon could be carried but only with heavy losses; the General, meanwhile, had made up his mind to attack through Mexicalcingo. On August 14, Scott informed his subordinates of his decision and ordered his division commanders to hold their troops in readiness. Shortly after this council of war broke up, the General abruptly countermanded his own order; word had reached him that one of Worth's officers had discovered another possible route, one that was practicable not only for infantry and cavalry but for artillery and wagons as well, south of Lakes Chalco and Xochimilco along the base of the mountains to San Augustin. Next day the advance by the new route was begun, and, on August 17, Worth's muddy veterans occupied San Augustin after brushing off the token force stationed there.

This flanking movement to San Augustin was one of the most important maneuvers made during the entire war. In one comparatively short march Scott had bypassed the strongest points in Santa Anna's exterior line of defenses and had placed his army in position to move against the city from the southwest or west, where the Mexican interior defenses were weakest. He had lifted the spirits of his own army while at the same time delivering a heavy blow to the enemy's morale by successfully turning their carefully constructed positions. Santa Anna, faced now with the necessity of improvising new defenses, moved rapidly in an effort to retrieve the situation. He hurried to San Antonio, a mile and a half north of San Augustin, to supervise defensive preparations personally. By moving guns and ammunition from the now useless position at El Peñon, he hastily converted that suburb into a formidable fortress. General Valencia's troops north of the city were also moved down and set to work erecting defenses in the theatened area.

From his position in San Augustin, Scott sent Worth's division north toward San Antonio to probe the strength of that approach. At the same time, his engineers were sent to reconnoiter the ground to the west in the direction of Contreras. While Worth was feeling his way northward, the engineers returned with the welcome news that it would be possible to cut a road through the rocky field directly west of San Augustin and gain access to the road leading into Mexico City through San Angel. When Worth reported strong enemy opposition at San Antonio, Scott again changed his strategy: instructing Worth to continue making a demonstration in front of San Antonio, he ordered the rest of the army to move westward and gain possession of the San Angel road. Scott now began his second major flanking movement of the Mexico City campaign, a movement that would ultimately bring about the battles of Contreras and Churubusco.

In anticipation of just such a maneuver, Santa Anna had ordered General Gabriel Valencia and his forces to the San Angel area and by the seventeenth of August the latter had marched southward and had taken up a defensive position near Contreras. On the following day, Santa Anna peremptorily ordered Valencia to retreat from his exposed position, an order that was wilfully disobeyed by the subordinate who, it must be admitted, proved more astute than his commander in correctly divining the American intention to bypass once again a position of real strength.

On August 19 the movement to flank the Mexicans at San Antonio began. While Worth feinted a thrust at that stronghold, Pillow moved with his troops through the lava field the Mexicans called Pedregal toward Contreras. Forced to build a road as they progressed and all the while harassed by enemy fire, Pillow's advance was painfully slow. But before nightfall he had moved one portion of his command into position in front of Valencia's camp and had sent the other wing of his command off to the right to occupy the village of San Geronimo. As darkness fell on the nineteenth, the issue was in grave doubt; both forces were in what could fairly be described as critical situations. The Americans, in occupying San Geronimo, had placed themselves in an excellent position to cut Valencia's supplies and communications or to attack him on the flank or in rear. On the other hand, their position began to look very much like a death trap when Santa Anna, just before dark, moved down from the north placing this isolated command in jeopardy in between two Mexican forces. Ironically enough, it was Santa Anna himself who saved the day for the Americans. After a short and ineffectual cannonade he withdrew, thereby passing up a wonderful opportunity to crush one detached wing of the invading army. Before pulling out, Santa Anna once again ordered Valencia out of the area, but when that officer contemptuously refused to obey, the commander moved off toward Churubusco leaving his rebellious subordinate to his fate.

During the miserable, rainy night of the nineteenth, the Americans at San Geronimo discovered a ravine leading to the rear of Valencia's position. When this intelligence was relayed to Scott at San Augustin a plan of attack for early next morning was speedily adopted: a diversion was to be made in Valencia's front while the main attack was to come at his rear. By three o'clock in the morning of the twentieth, the troops at San Geronimo were in motion, hoping to gain the Mexican rear by daylight. In order to deceive the enemy, a token force was left in the village with instructions to build fires and otherwise create the impression that the entire force was still there. Meanwhile, troops were also moved up directly on Valencia's front. At daylight, Mexican artillery opened up on the troops facing them, but, before this fire had time to become effective, the Americans struck unexpectedly and with force from the rear. The rout of the surprised Mexicans was complete: so demoralized were they that within seventeen minutes the engagement was over. In one of the most decisive battles of the campaign the American army, suffering losses numbering less than a hundred men, had once again inflicted a crushing defeat upon the Mexicans, taking a five to one toll in casualties. The Americans captured several generals, nearly eight hundred prisoners, twenty pieces of artillery, a large quantity of ammunition, and a number of mules. In this short engagement, fought early in the morning of August 20, the Mexican Army of the North was virtually shattered.

Upon receipt of the news of the rout at Contreras, Santa Anna, when he had issued instructions that Valencia was to be shot on sight, ordered the evacuation of San Antonio, which was now effectively outflanked, and concentrated his forces around the church and convent at Churubusco to await the next move of the invaders. In defeating Valencia, Scott had at last opened a road into Mexico City. Through Tacubaya he could now move directly against the capital, though this would entail the grave risks of allowing Santa Anna to remain on his right flank and separating the force moving onto the city from Worth's troops at San Antonio. Perceiving the disastrous possibilities in such a situation, Scott decided that before moving against the capital he must first occupy San Antonio and reunite his divided army. Ordering Worth to take possession of San Antonio, which was now being evacuated by the Mexicans, Scott concentrated the remainder of his army at Coyoacán to await developments.

The possibility of cutting off the evacuees straggling along the highway from San Antonio to Churubusco, however, spurred Scott into immediate action, and in an attempt to intercept them he moved hastily toward the latter position. At Churubusco, the American army ran into unexpected difficulties. Mexican sharpshooters from behind their solid defenses played havoc with the relatively unprotected assault force, and the Mexican artillery, manned by the notorious San Patricio Battalion of American deserters, was as accurate as at any time during the war. Churubusco was a hard-fought battle throughout, and the resolute Mexican defense was in no small measure attributable to the determination of the San Patricio deserters, who several times tore down with their own hands the white flags raised by the Mexicans. Not until late afternoon was the position finally carried and the issue settled with the bayonet. Scott's army, less than half as large as Santa Anna's defending force and wearied from the morning's fighting at Contreras, had successfully seized another strong position from the defenders. August 20, 1847, would go down in the Mexican calendar as a sad day. In the twin defeats of Contreras and Churubusco, Santa Anna lost a third of his effective troops through casualties, desertion, and capture, was driven from one of his few remaining strong points, and forced to fall back on his interior defenses. The Americans were now within three miles of Mexico City.

Despite these successes, Scott was forced to halt and rest his weary troops. Sickness, fatigue, discomfort, and lack of supplies plagued his scattered forces, and, although they were moving nearer to their prize, they still had to face the rugged line of interior defenses erected by the Mexicans for a last-ditch stand. The thousand casualties his dwindling army had suffered in the stubborn fighting on the nineteenth and twentieth further persuaded Scott against attempting an immediate assault upon the city. Giving his exhausted veterans a badly needed respite, the General sent in a demand for the city's surrender, underscoring his future intentions by deploying troops and establishing batteries from which to pound the capital in the event of a refusal.

Within Mexico City, meanwhile, all was confusion. Santa Anna, uncertain of his ability to repulse an attack with his dispirited soldiers, began adroitly to stall for time by sending back to Scott a feeler for peace and at the same time urging the American general not to advance for fear that such action would result in dispersing the Mexican government, thereby making any negotiation impossible. Scott, eager to begin peace talks, took the bait. On the morning of August 21 he forwarded a message to his cunning opponent stating that far too much blood had already been shed in "this unnatural war between the two great republics" and that it was high time their outstanding differences were honorably and amicably settled. In order to facilitate the opening of negotiations, Scott further expressed his willingness to sign "on reasonable terms" a short armistice. Santa Anna, skilfully capitalizing on Scott's unfortunate phraseology, eagerly (though insolently) accepted the offer and on the twenty-fourth of August both sides formally ratified the agreement. Under its terms hostilities were to cease: an armistice was agreed upon for opening peace negotiations, neither side was to reinforce or otherwise strengthen its position, prisoners were to be exchanged, and the Americans were authorized to procure supplies from the city under a flag of truce. Either side could terminate the armistice on forty-eight hours' notice.

In granting these terms, Scott unwittingly weakened his own position, relatively speaking, by giving his adversary a desperately needed breathing spell. Only the grumbling of the American troops, more suspicious apparently than their leader of Santa Anna's ingrained duplicity, disturbed the unnatural calm that settled over the area as the guns were, at least temporarily, silenced.

On the day following ratification of the armistice, diplomatic representatives of the two nations held the first in a series of fruitless meetings. Santa Anna needed time, and he bought it with this diplomatic pretense, though he was very careful to point out to the Mexican populace that, since perpetual war was both a calamity and an absurdity, he could not afford to overlook any means of securing an advantageous settlement. But even as the negotiators began their cautious sparring, other events occurred that more truly indicated the real Mexican temper. An American wagon train under precisely the sort of flag prescribed by the armistice, unarmed and without military escort, entered Mexico City to pick up stores for transportation to Tacubaya. Inside the city the train was attacked and driven back. Though he made not the slightest effort to put down the rioting when it occurred, Santa Anna did send an apology to Scott that the incensed American commander reluctantly accepted in an effort to prevent the collapse of negotiations. On the sixth of September the Mexican delegation expressed with finality their government's unwillingness to accept the demands made by the United States. The talks promptly ended. Scott, now thoroughly aroused at what appeared to him nothing less than deliberate treachery, angrily notified Santa Anna that he was terminating the armistice. The Mexican leader immediately sent a sharp reply to Scott and issued simultaneously an inflammatory proclamation to the inhabitants of the city expressing his determination to "preserve your altars from infamous violation, and your daughters and your wives from the extremity of insult." With this verbal explosion, the abortive armistice perished. It had worked altogether to the advantage of Santa Anna by granting him time, while carrying on specious negotiations with the invaders, to recover from the disasters of Contreras and Churubusco. During the two weeks thus gained, he had made careful preparations for giving the Americans a warm welcome when they should attempt to enter the city.

On September 7, Scott moved his army up to Tacubaya, from which the southwestern defenses of the capital could be assaulted. His engineers at this point reported two strong positions in this quarter: one was the frowning castle of Chapultepec, directly ahead, and the other, half a mile west of the castle, was a group of buildings known as Molino del Rey or King's Mill. These were in reality the two key positions in that area and so concerned was Santa Anna about their defense that he assumed personal command of them and made troop dispositions himself. Even though Scott's engineers had never been able to discover just how heavily these positions were reinforced, the American commander decided that he must first seize the Molino and destroy the guns which were being manufactured there for the defense of the capital. His opinion, strangely enough, was that there would be no serious opposition from the enemy.

The Battle of Molino del Rey, one of the bloodiest of the entire war, was fought early in the morning of September 8, 1847. After sending a force in the direction of the city, a successful feint that caused Santa Anna to rush some of his defenders back to protect the capital, Scott moved his main striking force off toward the west to take possession of the Molino. The first assault was against the southernmost buildings around which the left wing of the Mexican line had been concentrated. The first charge failed to dislodge the defenders, who forced the Americans to fall back under the pressure of their counter-attack. After a short breathing spell, a second charge was attempted, and this time the Americans reached the buildings and drove the Mexicans out. Next came an assault against the center of the enemy position, a stone building named the Casa Mata. Scott's infantry suffered heavy losses in a futile attempt to storm this strong position which eventually had to be reduced by artillery fire. On the extreme right of the Mexican line, a cavalry duel which ended when an American charge broke the Mexican line finished the fighting. By seven o'clock that morning, the battle was over; two thousand more casualties had been inflicted upon the Mexican army and seven hundred more prisoners taken. But it was at best a Pyrrhic victory for Scott's tiny army; the failure to determine the actual strength of the position was paid for by over seven hundred casualties, giving more than a little substance to the claim made by one officer that a few more such victories would ruin the army. Worse yet, the battle had actually been fought without a real objective, since only a few cannon were discovered in the foundry. All in all, the attack had been, as one American soldier described it, "a sad mistake."

With the capture of the Molino, it was inevitable that Chapultepec would be the next target of the American army, since the two routes leading from that direction into the city, one from the west by the San Cosme Gate and one from the southwest by the Belen Gate, were both swept by the guns of the palace that had once been the residence of viceroys but was now being used as a Mexican military school. Because of the terrain the castle was unassailable from the north, east, and southeast, but reconnaisance suggested the possibility of making a successful attack either from the south or southwest. Since his army had by now been reduced to around seven thousand effective troops and since there were two other routes leading into Mexico City from the south, Scott toyed for awhile with the idea of moving in by one of these alternate routes to avoid having to storm the palace. On September 11, he called a council of war and asked for the views of his officers. Lee of the engineers, supported by a number of other officers, argued in favor of advancing by one of the southern routes. But when another young engineer, P. G. T. Beauregard, presented a strong case for attacking from the west, Scott announced his decision to attack by the western gates. This meant, of course, that Chapultepec would have to be taken first.

Beginning early in the morning on the twelfth, a day's bombardment pounded the castle. Seeing that the Mexicans could not be driven from their position except by an assault, Scott ordered an attack for the next day and under cover of darkness moved his troops into position. By daylight on the thirteenth all was in readiness. Quitman's division was to attack from the south, Pillow from the southwest, and Worth from the extreme west. At 5:30 A.M., a cannonade was begun; at 8:00, the attack was made in force. In spite of a number of appalling mistakes, not the least of which was the failure to have scaling ladders in the proper place at the proper time, the Americans were able to take the castle after a bitter struggle. By 9:30 in the morning the Mexicans had surrendered the last major obstacle in the path of Scott's aggressive little army. The city of Mexico, the prize for which they had been fighting since landing on Mexican soil some six months earlier, now lay within their grasp. And they were eager to seize it. With scarcely a pause after the capture of the palace, the troops pressed on toward the gates of the city by both available routes: Quitman's division moved down the causeway leading to the Belen Gate while Worth's troops pushed on toward the San Cosme Gate.

Moving from arch to arch in the aqueduct to avoid the fire of Mexican gunners, Quitman's men gained possession of the Belen Gate shortly after noon. When they attempted to move further into the city, a Mexican counterattack pushed them back to the gate, where they were forced to fight with increased vigor merely to hold their position. Worth, in the meantime, arrived near the San Cosme Gate about four in the afternoon and finding the road there swept by a withering fire, reverted to the successful tactics of Monterrey. Sending his men burrowing through the walls of the adobe houses lining the upper side of the road until they reached a point in the rear of the enemy's position, he then ordered them up onto the top of a house commanding the Mexican batteries and, quickly lifting some howitzers into place, scattered the surprised defenders in all directions. By six o'clock Worth held the San Cosme Gate.

When night fell on September 13, both gates were in American hands. Even so, the position of the invading army was almost desperate. Reeling under the strain of the day's fighting that had cost another nine hundred American casualties, wearied by the morning assault and the afternoon's battering, low on ammunition and supplies and with their puny force divided in front of a numerically superior enemy, they still faced the difficult task of wresting the city, street by street and house by house, from its defenders. Fortunately for the Americans, Santa Anna again came to their rescue. With his army demoralized by defeat and the panicky civilian population rapidly getting beyond any hope of control, Santa Anna decided that the capital could not successfully be defended, and, as Worth turned his artillery upon the heart of the city, the dejected Mexican general departed with his troops for Guadalupe Hidalgo. Before daylight on the fourteenth, a delegation from the city appeared at Scott's headquarters in Tacubaya offering terms which the General curtly refused, since the city now lay at his mercy.

At dawn on the fourteenth of September, as Quitman was preparing to unleash his men for a final assault, another delegation approached under a flag of truce and surrendered the city. Advancing cautiously, Quitman occupied the Grand Plaza and at seven o'clock that morning raised the American flag over the Mexican capital. Within the hour Scott and his staff rode into the square warmed by the lusty cheers of the assembled troops. It had been little more than a month since this army had first looked down from the mountains upon the valley and city of Mexico. Such are the vagaries of war that this proud city was now to be ruled by a onetime professor of English, John A. Quitman, named by Scott as military governor of the city of Mexico.

The symbolic raising of the American flag over the enemy's capital did not, unfortunately, mean an immediate end to hostilities either in the city or the surrounding countryside. Scarcely an hour after Scott's arrival in the city, violence flared up. The trouble began when a group of American soldiers were fired upon just off the plaza; the rioting spread rapidly and by the end of the day the entire city was in turmoil. For three long days a pitiless, irregular warfare continued to

General Scott's Entrance into Mexico City

James K. Polk

rage in the city in spite of every effort of the city officials and clergy to stop it and of American troops to suppress it. The flat-roofed Mexican houses were ideal for guerrilla fighting. From their protected heights, snipers worked with deadly effect and those without guns hurled stones, broken bottles and miscellaneous objects on the troops below. Scott found it necessary to employ strong measures in order to regain control of the situation. Orders were issued to use artillery where necessary, armed patrols were sent against the mobs raging in the streets, and authority was given to enter any house from which a shot was fired. No quarter was to be given the inmates. By September 16 relative quiet had been restored. Under further orders, martial law was declared, guarantees were given the inhabitants for their persons, their property, and their religion, Mexican courts were kept in operation to hear routine cases and a local police force was enlisted to aid in keeping the peace. In spite of the General's levy of $150,000 on the city, within a very short time the stores were reopened, newspapers were being printed, entertainments of all kinds were being offered to American troops, and the saloons were doing a booming business.

Santa Anna had, in the meantime, fallen on evil days. His best efforts had ended in national disaster. In an attempt to pacify his political enemies and a hostile public he now resigned the presidency. Then in one last desperate gamble to restore his waning prestige the discredited Mexican leader moved with the remnant of his dispirited army to attack the American garrison at Puebla. The last ten days in September were spent in a boot-less effort to recapture Mexico's second city, but by the first of October, unable to force the Americans out of Puebla, he moved away toward Perote, reduced now to such pitiful straits that he could not even seize the enemy wagon train that was his objective.

On October 15, Santa Anna was relieved of his command and ordered to await the convening of a court-martial to investigate his conduct of the war. To his troops he made a farewell address in which he stated that he was sacrificing himself to the "vengeance" of enemies who had wanted him to accept an "inglorious peace." Santa Anna then formally turned over his command to a subordinate and, leaving the army, went into seclusion until the government finally banished him from the country. His removal to Jamaica by no means marked the end of his public career, however. During the 1850's he was again elected president of the republic even though he was out of the country. Two more years in office earned him another exile. The sixties witnessed another abortive return and in the seventies he finally came home to die after an incredible career that had spanned eighty tempestuous years.

Aside from the disturbances inside the capital and Santa Anna's last futile effort, the only fighting worthy of mention was the continuing series of attacks by irregulars or guerrillas on American wagon trains traveling from Veracruz to Mexico City. These attacks were neither organized nor supported by the Mexican government, and, since their purpose was to acquire booty rather than to repel invasion, they cannot fairly be counted part of the war.

The conquest of Mexico City was the decisive military campaign in the war with Mexico. The war in northern Mexico admittedly settled the long-standing argument over the boundary, and the war in New Mexico and California enabled United States troops to occupy territory that would soon after become part of the national domain; but it was this crushing blow at her vital center, resulting in the seizure and occupation of the capital that eventually brought the Mexican nation into submission and made possible the negotiation of a treaty of peace.

Nor is it enough merely to say that the Mexico City campaign was decisive. It was also brilliant. This first successful invasion of a foreign country by an American army was carried out in the face of crippling handicaps and seemingly insurmountable obstacles. Though plagued by internal dissensions, lacking the wholehearted support of the administration, outnumbered and forced to engage a superior adversary on unfamiliar terrain at places of the enemy's own choosing, Scott and his army nevertheless fought superbly. In the six months between their landing on the beach near Veracruz and the surrender of the capital, they had seized a base on the Mexican mainland, marched overland toward the capital driving the enemy from every position of attempted defense, bypassed the strong fortifications in front of the city, smashed the enemy at Contreras and again at Churubusco, seized the Molino del Rey and the castle of Chapultepec, and finally raised the American flag for the first time over a conquered enemy capital. Yet, strangely enough, this amazing feat failed to earn for Winfield Scott the place in history he clearly deserved as the ablest American commander between the Revolution and the Civil War.

V

Politicians and Generals

One of the thorniest problems facing a democratic nation at war is the maintenance of unity of purpose between civilian and military authority. Co-operation between the civilian leader and the military commander is obviously necessary if both are to attain their common objective—victory. When this civil-military relationship is cordial, when teamwork between these high officials is effective, the nation profits directly. In an atmosphere of mutual trust and confidence unnecessary friction is eliminated, and the total resources of the nation are more easily brought to bear against the enemy. But when this relationship is not friendly, when civilian authority and military authority are in conflict, the nation at war labors under an added handicap: the suspicion and distrust that is generated, the recriminations that are broadcast, the feuds that break out and the firings that inevitably follow—all make final victory more difficult.

In this country's history, the civil-military relationship has from the very beginning been conditioned by our fixed devotion to the tradition of civilian supremacy over the military. This tradition was firmly rooted in fear—fear of standing armies that had been used in the past and might be used again to suppress the liberties of the people. This fear was neither fanciful nor imagined; it had its origin in our English heritage and was greatly strengthened by our colonial experience. The Founding Fathers, when they created this government, specifically wrote into the new constitution the doctrine of civilian supremacy. Until recent times, this has remained a jealously guarded tenet of the American political system; and this helps explain why our professional officer corps has never produced a "man on horseback" and why we have avoided the temptation to become a "garrison state." Though we have historically been a people with a strong predilection for rewarding our military heroes with high public office, we have at the same time insisted that they then sever their military connections, shed their military trappings, and assume the posture of a retired soldier.

Within the framework of the United States government, both the civilian leader and the military commander have important responsibilities in time of war. Each has his own particular contribution to make to the war effort. The civilian leader is the elected head of the government and as such is charged by the people with primary responsibility to protect and defend the state they have temporarily entrusted to his care. Because of this responsibility, the political leader unavoidably becomes the policy-maker; it is he who must fix the political aims and objectives of the war as it is he who must bear the final responsibility for seeing that the war is carried to a successful conclusion. By virtue of his position and his obligation, the civilian leader, in determining policy, is influenced by military considerations, but he must take into account social, economic, and political pressures as well. The military commander is the agent or executor of the policy set by his civilian superior. Since he will be assigned the mission of carrying out that policy, it is desirable that he have at least an advisory voice in its formulation, but whether he is given this opportunity or not, he is nonetheless wholly an instrument of his government. The ideal solution of the civil-military problem is for each to contribute his peculiar talents: for the civilian leader, after considering the opinions of his subordinates, to formulate a positive policy; for the military specialist to translate that policy into military plans and to prosecute these vigorously.

Unfortunately, this ideal relationship is rarely achieved. In practice, quarrels between the civilian and soldier in wartime are frequent. Clashes of personality, conflicting political ambitions, the soldier's indifference to the politician's precarious position and his tendency to see things wholly in military terms, the ignorance of the civilian concerning military affairs, and the politician's preference for quick, cheap victories are all areas of controversy. The only way that civil-military friction can be minimized is for both parties to work carefully and patiently to avoid petty personal squabbles, to maintain a flexible policy, and to forego partisan politics. In our war with Mexico, none of these pitfalls was avoided. President Polk's relationship with his two most important military commanders, Zachary Taylor and Winfield Scott, left a great deal to be desired from the civil-military point of view. The differences in their respective personalities were so pronounced that conflict was perhaps inevitable. The President was a cold, reserved, and aloof person—a narrow-minded partisan who could be invincibly obstinate. Taylor was an outspoken old campaigner, frank to the point of bluntness, wilful, hard-bitten, and as stubborn in his own way as the President. Scott was domineering, vain, and pompous, greatly aware of his own abilities, and intolerant of any criticism, whether expressed or merely implied. In short, the three men were destined to clash.

These personality traits made it easy for them to quarrel among themselves, and quarrel they did. Sometimes they merely nagged one another over trivia, and sometimes they fought over important policy matters; but, whatever the immediate cause, the underlying basis for their conflict was politics. Polk was not just another Democrat; he was a dedicated and loyal party leader. His election and his subsequent declaration of war against Mexico inadvertently created a political dilemma for the President and his party. Since the Democrats were responsible for the nation's participation in the war, it was politically imperative that they win it if they hoped to stay in power. Yet the two most important military commanders, Taylor and Scott—the men most likely to reap political advantage from a successful war—were both Whigs. Unless something was done to destroy the political appeal of these two soldiers, the Democrats were faced with the unhappy prospect of having to win a war that seemed destined to make a Whig the next President of the United States.

Long before the "shooting war" with Mexico began, there was ample evidence of the President's distaste for the general he had ordered to the Rio Grande line. Polk not only disliked Taylor's political preferences, he also questioned his professional competence and repeatedly expressed grave doubts concerning his fitness for command. Had he been able to find a suitable replacement, Polk would undoubtedly have removed

Taylor from his command, for even in his more charitable moments the President felt serious misgivings: "He is brave but does not seem to have resources or grasp of mind enough to conduct a campaign. . . . He is, I have no doubt, a good subordinate officer, but from all the evidence before me I think him unfit for command. Though this is so, I know of no one whom I can substitute in his place." This animosity toward Taylor was in no way lessened in the early days of the war when the victories at Palo Alto and Resaca de la Palma and the subsequent occupation of Matamoros brought the General great public acclaim. Taylor's relations with the President grew worse as his own political star rose. Flattered by the suggestion that he might move from his tent into the White House, Taylor experienced a pleasant awakening of political ambitions at the very time the President began to feel the need to apply some kind of restraining pressure on the new popular idol.

The first skirmish between the two men occurred during the spring and summer of 1846 while Taylor's army was encamped along the Rio Grande line and was brought on by the General's repeated complaints against the government. In both his official and private correspondence, a new tone was noticeable; he complained of "extraordinary delays" in forwarding to him steamboats for use on the Rio Grande and petulantly wrote to his friends of a deliberate plot in Washington to keep him "in the dark." It was over the government's personnel policy, however, that he complained loudest. Each time the War Department wrote him urging that he curb the excesses committed by the volunteers under his command, Taylor wrote a lengthy reply condemning the policy of sending unmanageable and untrained boys into a foreign country to wage war. This nagging exchange of correspondence, while it did not lead to an open break between the General and the administration, did serve to keep alive the hostility that already existed between Polk and Taylor.

The rift between the two men finally occurred in the fall of 1846 as a result of the armistice granted the Mexicans at Monterrey. After forcing General Ampudia back into the heart of the city in September, 1846, Taylor on his own authority agreed to an eight-week armistice and allowed the Mexican army to retire from the city without even the formality of a parole. Taylor later attempted to justify this action on the grounds that his own troops were weary and demoralized and that his supply of provisions and ammunition was dangerously low. Since an assault was unlikely to meet with success and a retreat was unthinkable, Taylor settled for negotiations which gave him possession of the city at the cost of allowing the enemy army to withdraw in force.

On October 11, 1846, word of the armistice reached Washington, where it was immediately and roundly condemned by the administration. The President, who felt that Taylor had muffed a supreme opportunity to end the war with one smashing victory at Monterrey, wrote with obvious disappointment: "He had the enemy in his grasp and should have taken them prisoners. . . . It was a great mistake for General Taylor to agree to an armistice. It will only enable the Mexicans to reorganize and recruit so as to make another stand." Because he thought the General had violated his instructions, Polk refused to approve his course, and on the following day, after a cabinet meeting in which it was generally agreed that Taylor had committed a "great error," the President instructed his Secretary of War to order Taylor to terminate the armistice and resume the offensive. Marcy thereupon drafted the necessary orders, adding his own regrets that the General had not seen fit to demand a Mexican surrender. Upon receipt of this dispatch, Taylor hastily wrote an indignant reply in which he stated that the armistice had been granted "for considerations of humanity" as well as for sound military reasons. This inference of official callousness so incensed Polk that he seriously considered relieving Taylor of his command; no less informed an observer than Winfield Scott claimed that only Taylor's popularity saved him from the President's wrath. After this heated exchange, the two men grew increasingly cool toward each other. Polk was now confirmed in his earlier suspicion that Taylor was a blundering incompetent; the General was now confirmed in his suspicion that the President and his official family were conspiring to discredit him for political reasons.

Unfortunately, Taylor did not have to look far for signs of administration meddling. When the decision was made in Washington to occupy Tampico, a letter was sent to Taylor informing him not only of that decision but also of the fact that orders had been sent directly to General Robert Patterson, then at Camargo, to organize a force for the expedition. Infuriated by this official impertinence, Taylor wrote a scathing letter to the War Department protesting the manner in which a detachment had been made from his command and stating that if he was to be held responsible for military operations in that area then he must also have the right to organize the troops as he thought best and regulate the "time and manner of their service." "Above all," he insisted, "do I consider it important that the Department of War should refrain from corresponding directly with my subordinates, and communicating orders and instructions on points, which, by all military precept and practice, pertain exclusively to the general in chief command."

The interference of the War Department he denounced as a violation of the integrity of his command, a course "pregnant with the worst evils," and from which "confusion and disaster alone can result."

This outburst persuaded Polk that Taylor was not only incompetent but that he was also being deliberately unco-operative. Since Marcy's letters to both Patterson and Scott had made it abundantly clear that the orders were being issued directly to the subordinate commander only to save time, Polk concluded that Taylor was being unnecessarily touchy on this point because he wanted to further his political ambitions by engaging in an open quarrel with the administration. This suspicion, which had been growing in the President's mind for some time, was based primarily on the General's unwillingness to assume any responsibility in recommending campaign plans against the enemy. In spite of the President's expressed wish to occupy as much territory as possible in northern Mexico before the Mexican Congress met in December, 1846, Polk had gradually come around to the point of view that the northern campaign could never be really decisive because it was being fought too far away from the Mexican heartland. As early as July, 1846, queries were sent to the senior military commander on the scene in Mexico about possible alternatives. Taylor was told that the government was considering making an attack against Mexico City by way of Veracruz and was specifically requested to give his opinion of the proposed campaign. Answering with uncharacteristic evasiveness, Taylor stated that he might advance overland against the Mexican capital through San Luis Potosí, provided the government felt that ten thousand troops could be subsisted along that route. As for the Veracruz expedition, he simply refused to give an opinion, stating that any such decision would have to be made by the government.

Polk was understandably puzzled by the General's attitude and more than a little annoyed at what he pointedly described as the "want of reliable information." General Taylor, confided the President to his diary, "gives but little information. . . . He seems to act like a regular soldier, whose only duty is to obey orders." The General's reluctance to express an opinion or to accept responsibility seemed particularly unco-operative to Polk. The President complained bitterly that his general made no suggestions to the government even though he was in Mexico "with means of knowledge which cannot be possessed at Washington" and that he gave no information "to aid the administration in directing his movement." At the War Department's prodding, Taylor finally gave the government the benefit of his advice, though only in a negative way, by offering a number of choices. If the government planned to move against Mexico City from a port on the Gulf of Mexico, then Veracruz was in his opinion the best spot to make a landing. However, a more desirable policy, in his view, would have been to assume a defensive line in northern Mexico and force the Mexicans to drive them out. This policy, he argued, would shift the responsibilities and burdens of waging offensive warfare to the enemy and would give American troops the advantages of fighting on the defensive while occupying Mexican soil.

For some time, Polk remained undecided on what would be the best policy: whether to remain on the defensive in the north and wait for the enemy to open negotiations, or to move aggressively against Mexico City. The President instinctively disliked Taylor's defensive plan, since it threatened to create a stalemate. As a practical politician, Polk knew that he must either successfully terminate the war into which his administration had led the nation, or pay the supreme political price for failure to do so. Signs were everywhere mounting that the longer the war dragged on, the less popular it became at home. The recent elections had gone against the Democrats, a warning that prompted the influential senator from Missouri, Thomas Hart Benton, to call on his close friend in the White House and urge him to wage a more aggressive war against the enemy. The essentially defensive policy of holding territory already occupied could only "prolong the war and ruin the Democrat party," said Benton, who argued forcefully that because Americans were "a go-ahead people" the administration really had no choice but to secure a satisfactory peace or continue to press the war with boldness.

Under the pressure of necessity, then, and upon the counsel of his closest friends and advisers, Polk decided upon the Veracruz–Mexico City campaign as the best possible way to conclude the war. Convinced, however, of Taylor's unwillingness to co-operate with the administration, Polk was determined to find some other commander for this expedition, preferably someone more in sympathy with his policies. After a futile search for a deserving Democrat, he was finally forced to name another Whig, Winfield Scott, to the command, not because of confidence in his ability or his loyalty to the administration but because Scott was the one man in the army "who by his rank could command Taylor." The appointment of Scott, however else it might have been interpreted, was a direct slap at Taylor, and it emphasized the President's reluctance to pacify further the "narrow-minded, bigotted partisan" who had been "made giddy with the idea of the presidency."

The last lingering hopes for a reconciliation between the two men faded upon publication in the United States of a letter written by Taylor to an old army friend, General Edmund P. Gaines, in which he attacked the administration for its direction of the war. In vigorous style, he defended his original decision to grant an armistice at Monterrey and openly criticized the treatment that both he and his army had been accorded by the government. The letter was more than a catalogue of grievances against the administration. It was an outspoken attack upon the government's policy. If, wrote the General, this country was actually under the necessity of "conquering a peace," then he agreed that the Veracruz–Mexico City campaign was the only proper course of action. But, questioned Taylor, even if we should win the war by this means, would "the amount of blood and treasure which must be expended" be compensated for by the result? "I think not," he asserted, and in contrast to the administration's policy he again offered his own repudiated plan of holding a defensive line in northern Mexico and saying to the enemy, "Drive us from the country." Gaines showed this letter to a number of his personal friends, one of whom suggested that its contents be published. Gaines assented to this, and, after a perfunctory editing in which some of the confidential passages were deleted, the letter was given to a New York newspaperman and was published in early January, 1847.

Its appearance in the press caused a mild sensation, the most immediate result of which was the official condemnation of both generals—Taylor for writing it and Gaines for circulating it. Despite Gaines's vociferous denial that there was anything in the letter that could conceivably hurt the United States or benefit Mexico, Polk publicly denounced the letter as "highly exceptionable" and claimed that its publication was both "unmilitary and a violation of duty," since it broadcast the nation's war plans—plans that the government had "hoped to conceal from the enemy until they were consummated." At the President's behest, Secretary Marcy wrote a strongly worded letter to Taylor reprimanding him for exposing secret military plans: "Your letter will soon be in the hands of the enemy and should convey most valuable information to them," wrote the Secretary, who then proceeded to quote for the General's edification the army regulation providing "dismissal from the service" for any officer writing for publication "private letters or reports relative to military marches and operations" or for allowing such letters or reports to be published. Outraged at the "unfounded attack" on the administration, Polk ordered that the entire file of correspondence between Taylor and the War Department be published. "I regret," he said, the "necessity" for publishing the official record, but "a state of things has been produced by General Taylor which renders it necessary for the vindication of the truth and the good of the service." In less public utterances, the President unreservedly berated Taylor as a "vindictive and ignorant political partisan" who, in spite of the kindnesses and indulgence shown him by the administration, allowed himself to be controlled and managed by bad men for political purposes. Such was the feeling of the two men by this time that neither could bear to hear the name of the other mentioned.

The acceptance in Washington of the plan to launch the Veracruz expedition inevitably worsened an already bad situation. In order to carry out that operation, many of Taylor's troops in northern Mexico had to be transferred to Scott's command; Taylor concluded that Scott had joined in the administration's plot to ruin him. Sufficient troops were left

Taylor to occupy a defensive line in northern Mexico, an assignment derided by Taylor as stemming more from a desire to curb his popularity than to defeat the Mexicans. When suggestions were made in Washington that he abandon his advanced position at Saltillo and withdraw to Monterrey, the General stubbornly refused to act upon them. Rumor had reached him of a strong Mexican force moving in his direction, and the doughty old warrior had already decided to fight the oncoming Mexicans, "be the consequences what they may." When his military superior, General Scott, instructed him to withdraw to Monterrey, Taylor angrily replied that he intended to hold his present position unless "positively ordered to fall back by the government at Washington."

Although he was convinced that he had lost the confidence of the government which had "suffered" him to remain "ignorant of its intentions," Taylor nevertheless stated that, in spite of his personal mortification, he intended to carry out in good faith the policies of the administration even though, as he plaintively asserted, "I may be sacrificed in the effort." To the War Department he addressed a note regretting that the President had not thought it proper, when relieving so large a portion of his command, also to relieve the General "from a position where I can no longer serve the country with that assurance of confidence and support so indispensable to success." The bitterness in his heart he poured out in a letter to a personal friend: "We now begin to see the fruits of the arrangements recently made in Washington, by an intrigue of Marcy, Scott and Worth to take from me nearly the whole of the regular forces under my command while in the immediate front of the enemy. . . ." These, it must be understood, were the words of a man who had finally made the decision to allow his name to be used as a presidential candidate.

Polk was unshakable in his conviction that Taylor was an ingrate and a political dupe of "cunning and shrewd men of more talents than himself. . . ." Taylor, on the other hand, felt that the President, alarmed at his growing popularity, had deliberately and spitefully affronted him. When he intoned his favorite and oft-repeated pronouncement, "Evil men bear sway," he was not only referring to the President and General Scott, he also included almost all of official Washington with the possible exception of the Secretary of the Navy.

The last dreary scene in this drawn-out feud occurred just after the Battle of Buena Vista. Taylor's victory brought no congratulations from the President, who felt that the battle was unnecessary—that it should not and would not have been fought if Taylor had obeyed orders. The public adulation of Taylor seemed absurd to Polk, who felt that the General was a blundering old fool who had been saved by his men. "The truth is," commented the President uncharitably, "our troops, regulars and volunteers, will obtain victories wherever they meet the enemy. This they would do if they were without officers to command them higher in rank than lieutenants. It is an injustice," he added, "to award the generals all the credit." As a reprimand to Taylor, Polk refused to allow the army to salute the victory. The breakdown of relations was now complete. Taylor soon took a leave of absence from the army and returned home to a hero's welcome. In his eyes, his only mistake had been to win too frequently. It was his burgeoning popularity that had made him a political threat to the Democratic party and had ultimately cost him administration support.

"Polk, Marcy and Co.," he contended, have "been more anxious to break me down than to defeat Santa Anna." This was the theme that gained widespread popular support: an aged and courageous commander, victorious in spite of being stripped of his troops in the face of a powerful enemy. It was this image that made Taylor the next President of the United States.

Polk's personal and official dealings with his senior military officer, Winfield Scott, were fully as unsatisfactory as his relationship with the Hero of Buena Vista. The reasons for this lack of accord were essentially the same as those which plagued the Polk-Taylor association: conflicting personalities, policy disputes, and partisan politics. Scott's political ambitions had long been on display; in 1840 he had been one of the three most prominent contenders for the Whig nomination and in 1844 he had barely lost out to Henry Clay as the party's choice. As an active Whig politician, Scott was naturally in opposition to any Democratic candidate, but his distaste for their 1844 nominee was particularly strong because Polk had been hand-picked by the General's ancient enemy, Andrew Jackson. It was inevitable, on the basis of Scott's earlier opposition to Polk and the General's undisguised ambition for high office, that the President would feel some hostility toward him. Even so, this hostility was at least temporarily held in abeyance. In spite of his personal misgivings about Scott, whom he described as "scientific and visionary in his views" and despite his natural reluctance as a good Democrat to give command of the army to a Whig with political axes to grind, Polk appointed Scott to command on May 13, 1846. And though the President was not completely convinced that Scott was "in all respects suited to such an important command," he admitted that the General's position "entitled him to it if he desired it."

It was not long after the appointment that the first public quarrel between the two men erupted. Polk could see no justifiable reason for Scott's staying on in Washington. In the President's mind, the proper place for a military commander was in the field with his troops, not at a desk shuffling papers. Polk's impatience with what he considered military procrastination became a festering grievance. When he discovered that the General had no plans to leave for the Rio Grande before late summer, he huffily directed Secretary of War Marcy to confer with Scott and to warn him plainly that unless he left at once for the theater of operations, he would be superseded in command. This strained interview took place at an unfortunate time: Scott's pride had already been wounded by the implications of a recent Senate bill authorizing the appointment of two additional major generals for the army. Marcy's pointed comments rankled. They confirmed his suspicions that the bill was an administration measure aimed directly at him. Driven by fear and suspicion, Scott now made the tactical mistake of writing a grossly presumptuous letter to the War Department. Describing in great detail the duties that had kept him in Washington, he sarcastically stated his unwillingness to place himself in what he considered "the most perilous of all positions," that of having to endure a fire upon his rear, "from Washington," while facing the fire on his front "from the Mexicans." He concluded this remarkable letter, one of several he should never have written, stating that, since he did not enjoy the confidence of the government, the public interest demanded that he be replaced by another commander.

Polk's irritation at Scott's inactivity was increased by this impertinent letter which he saw on the same day he learned that Scott, in private correspondence, had charged that the new regiments about to be raised by the administration were to be Western Democrats and would not include Whigs, Easteners, or West Pointers. Concluding from these developments that Scott's "partisan feelings" were such that he was "unfit to be intrusted with the command," Polk hastily called a cabinet meeting to discuss the situation. In the opinion of the President's advisers, the General had at last gone too far. The Secretary of War, on May 25, informed Scott that he had shown his "extraordinary" letter to the President and that Mr. Polk considered certain obnoxious passages a direct assault upon the honor of the chief executive. When he had pointed out that the President had "in a frank and friendly spirit" intrusted Scott with a command upon which the glory of the country and the success of his own administration depended, Marcy took the General to task for imputing "unfair and illiberal motives" to the President and then relieved him of his command with these concluding words:

The President would be wanting in his duty to the country if he were to persist in his determination of imposing upon you the command of the army in the war against Mexico. . . . I am therefore directed by him to say that you will be continued in your present position here, and will devote your efforts to making arrangements and preparations for the early and vigorous prosecution of hostilities against Mexico.

This stinging rebuke was delivered to Scott during dinner on the evening of May 25, 1846. Shocked and surprised at such drastic and unexpected action, he hurriedly wrote a second letter attempting to rectify his earlier mistakes. But this frantic

letter was in a way worse than the first, for its clumsy phraseology made him the object of public ridicule. In opening, the
General described receiving the Secretary's letter as he was
having "a hasty plate of soup." He denied any intention of
charging either the President or the Secretary of War with
"unworthy motives." Praising the President's "excellent sense,"
his "military comprehension" and his other "admirable quali-
ties" and with an almost saccharine expression of gratitude to
the Secretary for the "many personal courtesies . . . received
at your hands," Scott humbly concluded his apology by affirming his readiness to do his duty either in Washington or, as he
preferred, along the Rio Grande.

This conciliatory effort was wholly wasted upon Polk, who
had become convinced that Scott had been vindictively in-
subordinate for political reasons. His refusal to reinstate Scott
was forwarded to that unhappy officer on June 2. The humiliation of the excitable and sensitive old soldier was now complete; stripped of his field command, publicly ridiculed as
"Marshal Tureen" as a result of his "hasty plate of soup"
phrase, Scott's mortification knew no bounds. There was more
than a little truth in the biting comment of one newspaperman
that the General had "committed suicide with a goose quill."

For the next three months, Scott continued quietly to per-
form his duties in Washington. Though privately he considered
himself disgraced, he studiously avoided any display of sullen-
ness or brooding. As early as September 12, he asked Marcy to
remind the President of his standing request for reinstatement
to command, a query that brought him this terse reply: "The
President requests me to inform you that it is not within the
arrangements for conducting the campaign in Mexico, to super-
sede General Taylor in his present command by assigning you

to it." The outlook for Scott was dark. There is little doubt that, but for two developments, he would have spent the rest of the war in relative obscurity behind a desk in Washington. These were, first, the adoption by the policy-makers of a new strategic plan of campaign and, second, Polk's failure to persuade Congress to create a billet for a lieutenant general of the army. This project was very dear to Polk's Democratic heart, for in it he saw the one possible opportunity of overshadowing his two Whig commanders. Polk felt confident that he had already discovered just the right man for that job. The man was, naturally enough, a Democrat: Thomas Hart Benton, United States senator from Missouri, who had earlier expressed to the President his willingness to serve in just such a capacity.

While these maneuverings were going on, plans were being readied for an advance against Mexico City by way of Veracruz. Polk, angered at Taylor's crankiness and uneasy over that General's growing popularity as a result of his victories in northern Mexico, reluctantly gave the new command to Scott in November, 1846. According to the President, the General was "so grateful and so much affected that he almost shed tears."

Scott's reinstatement marked the beginning of a brief period of co-operation and good will between the two men. In order to impress Polk with his co-operative spirit, Scott urged the President to name the volunteer generals to participate in the Mexico City campaign. He even used his influence on Capitol Hill to gain Whig support for certain administration war policies. When, at the end of November, Scott finally left Washington and moved to New Orleans to make final preparations for the attack, he was so convinced that he now enjoyed

Zachary Taylor

Battle of Buena Vista

the full confidence of the administration that he wrote impulsively to Marcy:

On setting out on my present mission I laid down *whiggism,* without taking up *democracy;* but without reference to party or politics, I have felt very like a Polk-man. At least the President has all my personal respect, sympathy & Esteem. I beg you to thank him for the kindness & the confidence he showed me.

This seeming rapport was deceptive. Even before he left New Orleans, Scott began to sense that there was no basis for a genuine reconciliation. When he first heard the rumor that Polk was attempting to make Benton a lieutenant general, Scott refused to believe it; but his old anxieties and fears were once again aroused when he learned from a trustworthy source that the President, since his departure, had criticized him for spending too much time in New Orleans and for making "extravagant" preparations for the campaign.

In such a tense atmosphere, trouble was bound to recur, as it soon did. This second flare-up between the two men arose over an incident involving Colonel William S. Harney, an officer of the dragoons. Harney, who had served with Taylor in northern Mexico, was ordered to join Scott's command for the Veracruz expedition. Scott, feeling that Harney was personally hostile to him, ordered him to rejoin Taylor, but the impulsive colonel, eager for his share of the glory about to be won, refused to obey Scott's order. In the face of such obvious insubordination, Scott had no alternative: he court-martialed Harney. But after the court found the colonel guilty and ordered that he be reprimanded in general orders, Scott, hoping to smooth over the affair, remitted the sentence and generously allowed Harney to accompany the expedition. When news of this incident reached Polk, however, he immediately jumped to the conclusion that the affair really had a political basis. Convinced that the action against Harney had been taken solely because he was a Democrat, Polk abruptly countermanded Scott's earlier order that had relieved Harney of his command. This letter of rebuke reached Scott just after his capture of Veracruz. Their truce was now over.

While the General was still disturbed over the Harney incident, he learned for the first time of the arrival in Mexico of Mr. Nicholas Trist, chief clerk in the Department of State, who had been selected by Polk to negotiate a peace with Mexico. Trist was an old Washington hand; he had married a granddaughter of Thomas Jefferson and served as private secretary to Andrew Jackson; he had also had limited diplomatic experience as resident consul in Havana, where he had gained a fair knowledge of the Spanish language. Trist was sent to Mexico to travel with Scott's army in order that the government might be prepared to negotiate any time the Mexicans felt so inclined. Among his possessions he carried a draft of the proposed treaty and a sealed letter from the Secretary of State to be forwarded to his Mexican counterpart. The Secretary of War, in the meantime, wrote General Scott of Trist's mission and directed the General to forward to the appropriate parties the sealed proposal of the Secretary of State. This note annoyed Scott, but he succeeded in holding his tongue until Trist, upon his arrival at Veracruz, wrote an unfortunately worded letter to Scott assuming a tone that the General found extremely offensive. Scott again turned from the sword to the pen and wrote an intemperate letter to Trist in which he impugned the motives of the President, of the Secretary of

War, and of Trist himself. Trist immediately returned an insolent rejoinder that completely alienated the soldier and the diplomat before they had even met. To the outraged General, the situation now seemed altogether intolerable. Not only had the administration flaunted its lack of confidence in him by sending a sealed dispatch for forwarding, they had further insulted him by sending to his army a representative of the State Department with a quasi-independent status. This was more than the irascible old soldier could bear. Just how deeply he was offended was revealed in the petulant letter he dashed off to the Secretary of War:

Considering the many cruel disappointments and mortifications I have been made to feel since I left Washington, or the total want of support or sympathy on the part of the War Department which I have so long experienced, I beg to be recalled from this army the moment that it may be safe for any person to embark at Vera Cruz, which I suppose will be early in November.

Back in Washington, meanwhile, the President and his advisers, irritated by the unseemly squabble, toyed for awhile with the idea of recalling them both. Other considerations, primarily military ones, prevented this, but letters of reprimand were sent to each of them. Scott and Trist, in the meantime, had not only reconciled their differences, they had become fast friends. Their letters back to Washington were thick with praise for each other; each man now claimed all the blame for having misjudged the character and motives of the other. But though the reconciliation between Scott and Trist was complete, the break between the General and the President was never healed. As far as Scott was concerned, the administration had demonstrated a despicable deceitfulness. Not only had it failed to provide the promised support, it had also deliberately humiliated him in the Trist affair. For this discourtesy he never forgave Polk.

The high point in this feud between the President and his senior field commander was reached as a result of Scott's quarrels with some of his own officers. After the capture of Mexico City certain newspapers in the United States carried unofficial accounts of the campaign highly uncomplimentary to Scott and emphasizing the contributions of Generals Pillow and Worth. This blatant violation of army regulations caused Scott to issue a stern general order on November 12, 1847. In it, Scott declared that it required not a little "charity" to believe that the "principal heroes" had not written these accounts or had them written; he added, pointedly, that "the intelligent can be at no loss in conjecturing the authors—chiefs, partisans and pet familiars." Upon publication of this order, General Worth wrote an indignant letter which he sent to the President through Scott. Scott, after reading the letter, immediately placed Worth under arrest for insubordination. General Pillow was subsequently placed under arrest on a similar charge.

Polk was angered by this "persecution" of his onetime law partner. He was generally disgusted with this "most embarassing state of things" which he felt had been brought about wholly by Scott's "bad temper, dictatorial spirit and extreme Jealousy lest any other Gen'l Officer should acquire more fame in the army than himself." In retaliation, the President dismissed the charges against Worth and ordered that officer's release as well as Pillow's. He then ordered a court of inquiry to investigate the charges made against General Scott! Nor was this all: as a crowning blow, Polk peremptorily removed Scott from his command in Mexico City and replaced him with

Politicians and Generals

General William O. Butler, whose qualifications for the job were that he had served with Jackson in the War of 1812, was a veteran of the Monterrey campaign and—not the least in importance—was a registered Democrat!

One last indignity was still to be heaped upon Scott by the administration. But Scott was so crushed by the President's ingratitude in relieving him of his command that he endured the tedious court of inquiry with resignation that bordered on despair as it dragged on throughout the spring and summer of 1848.

Though Scott had been roughly handled by the administration, this treatment neither broke his spirit nor ruined his career. Within a short while, he began to recover from the damaging blows he had received, and, as his sagging spirits revived, his denunciation of Polk became more vitriolic. In later days, the General was ever willing to express contempt for Polk's "odious character," "cunning" and "hypocrisy." Despite these troubles, Scott's army career was relatively unaffected: he was brevetted a lieutenant general in 1852 and remained the dominant personality within the army until after the outbreak of the Civil War. Even his political fortunes survived, and though he was passed over by the Whigs in 1848, he was finally nominated for the presidency by his party in 1852, only to be defeated in the campaign by a former subordinate in the Mexican War, Franklin Pierce.

The Mexican War is a case history of poor civil-military relations. The lack of unity between high civilian and high military authority produced the same undesirable results in that war that it always had and perhaps always will. These unnecessary frictions prevented co-operation where it was desperately needed. Valuable time and vast energies were wasted, the pressing problems facing the government-at-war were unnecessarily multiplied.

In retrospect, conflict between the politician and his two generals appears to have been inevitable—not so much for reasons of personality or policy but for reasons of politics. For even if Polk, Taylor, and Scott had been able to reconcile their personal differences and had agreed on recruitment policies, on campaign plans, and on armistice terms, their attempt to co-operate would ultimately have foundered on the rock of partisan politics. Even if Polk could somehow have found it possible to forgive his two generals for their past political activities, his deep sense of loyalty to his own party would sooner or later have brought him into conflict with them because of their future political aspirations. For all his avowals that he had been "wholly uninfluenced" by the political opinions and associations of the army officers, Polk was from the beginning of the war caught in a web of political circumstance that made it impossible for him to look with favor upon either of his two most prominent generals.

Thus, it was politics that consistently frustrated any real co-operation. It was politics that created in the minds of the generals their suspicions that the President was deliberately trying to ruin them. It was politics that drove Polk to connive at such devious means of overshadowing them as his abortive maneuver to elevate Benton and his short-lived sponsorship of another soldier-Democrat, Robert Patterson, which abruptly ended when it was discovered that Patterson was not a native American and therefore could not become President. It was politics that created and sustained this ironic situation wherein a

Politicians and Generals

Democratic President was faced with the awesome task of having to win a war with two Whig generals without in the process allowing either of them to acquire sufficient luster to bring about the defeat of the President's own party in the next election.

VI

The Hidden War

One of the more curious features of the American military experience has been our propensity to fight two wars simultaneously; one against the common enemy and another among ourselves. In addition to our fight against a foreign foe there has usually been another war, a hidden war, going on behind the scenes, an internal struggle that has been as interesting as the fight against the outsider. This hidden war, waged exclusively within the American military establishment, is a result of certain inter-service and intra-service quarrels. It is fought on three major fronts and involves our generals versus our generals, our army versus our navy, and our regulars versus our volunteers. And while the face of war is never pretty, this particular brand is especially repugnant not so much because it threatens the nation's security as because it is a shameful story of pettiness, vanity, personal ambition, and professional jealousy. Yet this story recurs in American history; its causes are rooted in this nation's traditions and policies.

The Hidden War

The paltry guerrilla warfare that is carried on by high-ranking military officers among themselves stems partly from professional pride and partly from personal opportunism. Whatever a declaration of war might mean to an officer personally, it provides him professionally with the opportunity to excel at the thing for which he has been specifically trained. For the career officer, the battle is unquestionably the payoff. And since it is in wartime that military reputations are made, it is in wartime that the keenest competition among military men is aroused. This competition easily degenerates into bitterness and enmity when personal or political ambitions are at stake. In the United States, this danger has been increased by our penchant for rewarding military heroes with the highest office in the land.

Squabbles between the army and the navy have seemingly been as unavoidable as the bickering among brass hats. As long as the sister services act independently of one another, their relationship remains relatively smooth. Each seeks its own version of glory by carrying out its assignments under the undisputed command of one of its own officers. But when they are called upon to act in concert, friction is generated, a friction that usually results from the lack of unified command. The joint operation, where the two services work in close proximity, has historically been a fruitful field for inter-service controversy.

Hostility between the regular soldier and the volunteer soldier in the United States army was always apparent in the wars of the nineteenth century and was the inescapable result of a military policy adopted early in the nation's history: the maintenance of a small regular army, for policing our borders and preventing domestic insurrection, around which a larger volunteer army could be built in time of war. This policy was directly responsible for the cleavage between the regular and the volunteer. Whenever war has come, great masses of untrained or partially trained volunteers have been enlisted and placed alongside regulars already on duty. The regular soldier looks upon the volunteer as a careless, undisciplined amateur. Not unnaturally he resents this invasion of his well-ordered world by piddling incompetents who spend most of their time enthusiastically disrupting the routine. The volunteer, on the other hand, resents what appears to be an unnecessary and sometimes oppressive discipline. He is bored with army routine and is quick to remind the regulars that the peacetime army is merely a garrison force, that when war does come, it is the citizen-soldier who is relied upon. This mutual contempt is freely expressed by both groups.

In the war with Mexico, the American military establishment was plagued by all three of these problems. Quarrels among high-ranking officers were all too numerous; army-navy amity was severely strained; the regulars and the volunteers were at each other's throats. It is no exaggeration to say that one of the really important problems posed by the war was that of keeping the Americans fighting Mexicans rather than each other.

The two most prominent American soldiers in the Mexican War, Winfield Scott and Zachary Taylor, became in the course of that conflict bitter personal enemies. In spite of their obviously different personalities, the two men might well have remained on friendly terms had they not both been bitten by the presidential bug. Taylor's early victories on the Rio Grande line exuded the sweet smell of success that brought the professional politicians swarming to his camp and marked the beginning of Scott's political eclipse by his subordinate officer. When Scott later superseded Taylor in command in the field, Taylor, suspicious by nature, was convinced that his superior had joined a hostile administration in a deliberate effort to discredit him. He therefore severed all personal connections with the commanding general.

In the early days of the war, their relationship was a cordial one. Scott, in Washington, wrote promptly to congratulate Taylor for his "great and brilliant victories" at Palo Alto and Resaca de la Palma, and, if the commanding general felt any twinges of jealousy in the months following, he suppressed them. He could in all truth write to his field commander that he continued to watch over his interests and his fame with "the liveliest solicitude." Such protestations of good faith were convincing to Taylor, who at this time wrote reassuringly to a friend that General Scott was favorably disposed toward him "on all occasions." This mutual confidence was short-lived, however, for in November, 1846, as a result of the administration's adoption of new strategic concepts and of the President's personal dislike for Taylor, Scott was named to command the Veracruz expedition. Upon receipt of orders, Scott wrote what was for him an unusually tactful letter to Taylor again praising that general's accomplishments in northern Mexico and informing him of the government's decision. "I shall have to take most of your troops," he wrote; but, since he knew this loss would be "infinitely painful" to Taylor, Scott offered to meet him at Camargo in December to discuss fully with him the administration's new policy.

These new developments came as a stunning blow to Taylor. When Scott journeyed to Camargo for the proposed meeting,

Taylor pointedly arranged to be unavailable. In a bitter letter to Scott, he expressed his belief that he should have been relieved of his entire command. He added, petulantly, that, in spite of the fact that he had lost the confidence of the government, he remained determined to do his best, though he personally might be "sacrificed" in the effort. From the moment Taylor received Scott's letter about the new plan (he described it to a close friend as "a contemptible and insidious communication") his hatred for Scott was almost pathological. On various occasions he described Scott as a "humbug," called him an intriguer who had "wormed" himself into command, and charged that his own humiliation had been deliberately brought about by "Scott, Marcy & Co." Scott unquestionably sensed this animosity and even began to react to it by belittling Taylor's military achievements, as, for example, in his reference to Taylor's capture of the "little village" of Monterrey. By the autumn of 1847, the rupture was complete. "Between ourselves," wrote Taylor to his son-in-law, "General Scott would stoop to anything however low and contemptible . . . to obtain power or place. . . ." To a friend, he stated with an air of finality: ". . . he and myself now understand each other perfectly, and there can for the future be none other than official intercourse between us."

The low esteem in which the two leading generals held one another was in each case shared by a number of other officers as well. While Taylor was still encamped at Corpus Christi, critics among his subordinate officers began the verbal sniping that continued throughout the war. One subaltern wrote that the army had not "the slightest confidence" in the General's abilities; another prophesied shortly after reporting for duty: "If Taylor succeeds, it will be by accident." Before he had an opportunity to engage the Mexicans, Taylor lost at least temporarily the services of one of his officers, William Jenkins Worth, as a result of a dispute over rank. The commander's obvious reluctance to hand down a firm ruling on the question of the superiority of brevet rank (rank higher than that for which the officer receives pay) caused Worth to leave the army in disgust. Though Worth returned in time for the Monterrey campaign, Taylor fought the early phase of the war without this able officer.

Even those early victories at Palo Alto and Resaca de la Palma that had made Taylor the darling of the American public failed to squelch criticism of him within the army. His apparent lack of military knowledge seemed appalling to some officers; Lieutenant George Gordon Meade commented unkindly on the General's "perfect inability" to make use of his intelligence. Another and less tactful officer bluntly stated that Taylor was "utterly, absurdly, incompetent." But the sharpest criticism of Taylor's generalship followed the Battle of Monterrey and was specifically directed at the attack on the eastern end of the city that had been under Taylor's personal direction. His conduct of this assault was variously described by officers under Taylor's command as "rash," "headlong," and "injudicious." One young West Pointer heatedly claimed that the Monterrey casualties were nothing less than a sacrifice to "the blind folly and ignorance" of the commander. Taylor's second-in-command stated that the troops at Monterrey had been "murdered." In a letter home, General Worth frankly questioned "whether an idea strategic or of any description had had the rudeness to invade the mind or imagination of our chief" adding that the army in Mexico was "literally a huge body without a head."

Nor was Scott any more fortunate than Taylor in this respect. As long as he remained in Washington, the general-in-chief managed to keep fairly free from squabbles with his brother officers. But when he moved into active command in the field, he immediately encountered difficulties with his subordinates. The first clash came when he learned that W. S. Harney, an officer attached to Taylor's command, had been ordered to join the Veracruz expedition. Scott, acting on the knowledge that Harney was personally hostile toward him, ordered him back to northern Mexico. Harney refused to go, was court-martialed, and found guilty, but Scott, in reviewing the case, remitted the sentence and allowed him to accompany the expedition.

His quarrels with his division commanders during the campaign against Mexico City were extremely bitter. David Twiggs was, in Scott's opinion, unfit to command an army "either in the presence or in the absence of the enemy"; Gideon Pillow was placed under arrest following the controversy over the unofficial accounts of the capture of Mexico City. But by all odds the most rancorous dispute was with Worth, Scott's close personal friend for over thirty years. Worth had served on Scott's staff in the War of 1812 and again in the Black Hawk War and the warmth of his feeling for Scott was shown in 1840, when he named his son Winfield Scott Worth. In the Mexican War, Worth first served in the northern theater of operations. His dislike for Taylor sharpened the satisfaction he felt when he received orders to join his old friend Scott in the strike against Mexico City. His satisfaction was short-lived, however. The long-standing personal friendship between the two men ended long before they reached the Mexican capital.

The Hidden War

The first signs of trouble appeared shortly after the Battle of Cerro Gordo. Scott's official report, in which Twiggs's actions were given surprisingly high praise, infuriated the ambitious Worth, who had earlier been annoyed by Taylor's deliberate effort to withhold proper recognition for his exploits during the campaign in northern Mexico. Lashing out angrily at his old friend, Worth denounced the report as "a lie from beginning to end."

From that moment, Scott and Worth drifted further apart. The breach became irrevocable during the occupation of Puebla, when Worth, upon entering the city, agreed with local authorities to allow Mexican laws to remain in force. Scott, having in the meantime placed American soldiers in Mexico under martial law, was forced to revoke Worth's order, once again irritating his unduly sensitive subordinate. Later in the occupation, General Worth committed another error in judgment when, as a result of his fears of a Mexican uprising, he issued his famous "Poison Circular" alerting his men with the unflattering suggestion that the Mexicans, "as is the habit of cowards" might attempt "to poison those from whom they . . . fly in battle." Promulgation of this circular not only outraged Mexican public opinion, it also annoyed General Scott, who immediately demanded its withdrawal. Worth thereupon demanded a court of inquiry, and in spite of the fact that Scott handed him the mildest of rebukes, Worth, from then on, remained his implacable enemy. Worth's smoldering resentment once more burst into flame upon publication of his commander's official report of the capture of Mexico City. And Scott actually changed the report in an effort to soothe Worth's feelings. As a matter of fact, Scott had intended Worth to have the honor of occupying the enemy capital, hoping thereby to pacify him, but Worth's ungovernable temper prevented any such reconciliation.

The final disintegration of this lifelong friendship came when Scott learned that Worth was also inplicated in the "Leonidas" letter, an attack upon his generalship published under a pseudonym. He hastily issued a blistering rebuke in a general order which so provoked Worth that he wrote to President Polk through his commanding officer an intemperate letter which was so offensive that Scott placed his subordinate under arrest. Worth's hatred for Scott was obvious in the court of inquiry that followed. Later on, he legally changed the name of his son to William Scott Worth.

In the course of the war, then, the two senior field commanders were alienated not only from each other but from a number of other officers as well. In every major theater of the war, the conquest of Mexico was accompanied by a disgraceful squabbling among American officers. The heated denunciations, reprimands, courts of inquiry, and courts-martial left behind a trail of broken friendships and bitter hatreds. This bickering might have seemed ludicrous or merely wearisome had it not tended to weaken, disrupt, and divide a hard-pressed army operating in the very heart of the enemy's country.

During the early days of the war—indeed throughout its entire course—the Gulf Squadron was afflicted with none of the bitter inter-service rivalry found in the Pacific. By early May, 1846, Commodore Conner had concentrated his vessels off Point Isabel, near the mouth of the Rio Grande, to offer support to Taylor's army. When the Mexicans made a demonstration against the installation at Point Isabel (flatteringly called

Bombardment of Veracruz

Major General Winfield Scott

Fort Polk by the army), Conner promptly landed five hundred sailors and marines to help defend the post. This action earned a warm note of thanks from the army for "support and co-operation from a kindred branch of the public service." This auspicious beginning was soon followed by other examples of co-operation. As Taylor moved along the Rio Grande line through Reynosa and Camargo toward Monterrey, the navy supported the advance by transporting men and material up the river. Along the Mexican Gulf Coast, the two services acted in concert on several occasions to capture key ports. One such joint expedition called for a simultaneous attack by land and water against Alvarado. When a zealous young naval lieutenant succeeded in capturing the town before the army units arrived on the scene, the navy was so embarrassed that it ordered a court-martial for the conqueror. This act unquestionably marks the high point of army-navy camaraderie in this or any other war.

But by far the best example of army-navy co-operation was the Veracruz expedition. Both Conner and his successor, Matthew C. Perry, were eager to lend a hand to the ground forces. Scott and Conner worked particularly well together, with the Commodore advising the General on selection of a suitable landing beach below Veracruz as well as exercising general supervision over the landing. Conner commended his sailors for their "zealous and energetic" work and reported to his superiors in Washington that the navy had done everything in its power to contribute to the success of the operation. As soon as the men whom he enviously described as his "more fortunate brethren" in the army had established a beachhead, Conner sent several navy working parties ashore to help construct gun emplacements in preparation for the siege.

While the city was under assault, Conner was replaced by Commodore Perry, who pursued the co-operative course set by his predecessor. When Scott asked for navy guns to help breach the walls of the city, Perry agreed to put them ashore provided his men should be allowed to man them. Though the General was somewhat reluctant to acquiesce in this arrangement, he eventually did so under pressure of necessity. The guns were transferred ashore along with a detachment of sailors and marines, while ships in the harbor kept up a bombardment of the formidable castle of San Juan de Ulúa and maneuvered whenever possible to draw fire from the city, thus diverting it from the land forces. Scott expressed his appreciation in a generous letter to the naval commander thanking him and his "brothers of the navy" for their support; in fact, so pleased was the General with the navy's work that in his plan to storm the city he assigned one assault column to the sailors and marines. This operation never materialized, however, because the Mexicans surrendered the city before the planned assault was launched.

With the capitulation of Veracruz, the bond between the services began to dissolve. Petty dissensions broke out almost immediately. A representative of the navy attended the surrender ceremony acting independently of the army, and when Scott issued his official report of the capture of the city, Perry, claiming that the city had surrendered to both the army and the navy, protested the failure of the General to mention the important role played by the navy in the operation. Scott, having no wish to offend the navy, forwarded a formal apology to the navy and also amended his report by inserting the word "navy" after "army" in appropriate places. Later on, while en route to Mexico City, the General finally lost his temper with the navy when Lieutenant Raphael Semmes arrived at his headquarters requesting an escort for his mission to inquire about naval prisoners held by the Mexicans. Scott curtly refused the young officer's request but allowed him the privilege of remaining and traveling with the army if he so desired. In spite of these minor irritations, army-navy co-operation in both northern and central Mexico was more than adequate.

Such was not the case in California, however, where the peculiarities of the theater of operations required almost continuous inter-service co-operation. The authorities in Washington were obviously aware of these possibilities for conflict. President Polk issued an emphatic statement that he expected, indeed required, cordial and effective co-operation between officers of the two services. He made it unmistakably clear that he would hold to strict accountability any officer who failed to work harmoniously with members of the other service. In a further effort to head off serious bickering, the naval commander of the Pacific Squadron was pointedly elevated to rank equivalent to that of major general in the army.

As early as June, 1845, instructions had been forwarded to Commodore John D. Sloat, commander of naval forces off California, to blockade the coast should war be declared. When news of war finally did reach the squadron in early July, 1846, Sloat temporarily shook off his infirmities and his indecision long enough to occupy Monterey. He was planning further operations when his relief, Commodore Robert F. Stockton, arrived on the scene and assumed command. This change in command was destined to have a direct bearing on the conduct of the war in California. It signified the replacement of an aged, ailing, "old navy" man who thought a sailor's proper place was aboard ship by an ambitious and aggressive officer who felt no reluctance about taking his sailors ashore. The accession of Stockton precipitated the first crisis in army-navy relations in California, for now both services in that area were commanded by unusually active men, Stockton afloat and John C. Frémont ashore. These two interesting officers worked out a *modus operandi* during a personal conference. Under Stockton's authority, Frémont was to exercise tactical command of a mixed force of soldiers, frontiersmen, sailors, marines, and United States citizens living in the area. This motley group, officially named the California Battalion, carried through the conquest, and later the reconquest, of California. The arrangement seemed satisfactory to both officers: Frémont had his command, yet Stockton could continue to consider it more or less an extension of his naval command.

The precarious balance that Stockton and Frémont had so carefully arranged was upset by the arrival in California of General Stephen W. Kearny from New Mexico. In a comic sequence of events, Stockton offered to step down and turn the supreme command over to Kearny in deference to his rank. But Kearny, having only recently arrived in the area, refused. Stockton continued in charge under the old arrangement, but an increasing tension between the Commodore and the General soon became evident. It was brought into the open when Stockton refused Kearny's request for appointment as civil governor of California. This position Stockton had already given to Frémont, who was considerably junior in rank to Kearny. Nor was the situation in any way improved by Kearny's annoying habit of offering unsolicited advice to Stockton on military movements. Even so, when on the eve of the second attack on Los Angeles General Kearny suddenly changed his mind and insisted that he be given command of the expedition,

Stockton yielded to the point of allowing him to command
the infantry.

After the city was occupied for the second time and military
activities in California subsided, Kearny renewed his demand
that Stockton turn over the command to him. The Commodore, who by this time was most anxious to return to sea, began
putting his affairs in order. His decision to appoint Frémont
governor of California was so vehemently objected to by
Kearny that Stockton peremptorily suspended the General from
command of United States forces in the area. Just how strained
the feeling among American forces in California had become
was reflected in Kearny's bitter reply to Stockton: "I must,"
he wrote, "for the purpose of preventing a collision between
us and possibly a civil war in consequence of it, remain silent
for the present, leaving with you the great responsibility of
doing that for which you have no authority and preventing
me from complying with the President's orders." In spite of
the General's protest, Stockton did appoint Frémont to the
post. In August, 1846, Stockton, accompanied by his "maritime
army," boarded his vessels, leaving behind in California confusion bordering on anarchy.

Ashore, the stage was now set for a showdown between
Kearny and Frémont. When instructions arrived from Washington designating Kearny as military commander in California,
the General's first act was to depose his junior officer and send
him back to Washington to face trial. A court-martial found
him guilty of "conduct prejudicial to good order and discipline" and sentenced him to be dismissed from the service, a
punishment of such severity that it gave rise to the charge that
Frémont was being "sacrificed" by the army because of his
"deference" to an officer of the navy. President Polk, partly

out of respect for Frémont's political connections—he was the son-in-law of Senator Thomas Hart Benton—remitted the sentence of the court. Frémont, in disgust, resigned his commission anyway.

For years after the war, the argument was carried on by officers in each service about the relative importance of their respective roles in the conquest of California. President Polk seemingly gave a slight edge to the navy in his statement that the Pacific Squadron "with the cooperation of a gallant officer of the army" had secured California for the United States. In a more partisan vein, the Secretary of the Navy claimed that the conquest of California had from necessity "devolved" upon the navy, because there was no real military force in the area. The navy's claim was based on the fact that Commodore Stockton conceived, directed, and executed the general plan of campaign by which California was secured.

In order to understand clearly the causes of army-navy friction in the Mexican War, one must grasp the fact that it was essentially the army's war. Mexico had no navy to speak of. It was evident to United States naval officers from the very beginning that there would be no chance for a repetition of those exciting duels at sea that had thrilled the nation in the War of 1812. Except in the California campaign, the navy's role in the war was restricted to the performance of dull, plodding tasks—transporting men and supplies and enforcing the blockade. Partly, perhaps, in compensation for these inherent restrictions, the navy sought ways to participate in the war on land and in doing so increased the possibilities for interservice conflict. The Gulf Squadron and the army, primarily because of the good sense of the two commanding officers, avoided any serious dispute. But the Pacific Squadron's amphibious activities proved disastrous for army-navy relations. The Mexican War, particularly in the California theater of operations, made this lesson unmistakably clear: Lack of unity of command leads to quarreling which eventually destroys effective co-operation between the two branches of the service, damages the morale of the men in each and thereby sacrifices the best interests of the nation.

Hostility between the regulars and the volunteers in the Mexican War was even more persistent than that between the army and the navy. And this hostility was by no means confined to the enlisted ranks. Officers of the regular army were understandably discouraged when untrained civilians were given higher rank than their own, and they were quick to criticize the shortcomings of these "political generals." One officer, having been associated with Generals Patterson, Pillow, and Quitman, wrote home that he had seen enough of them "to be well satisfied that all their sense of justice and ambition lies in advancing the interest of their party and gaining some capital for themselves." One West Pointer characterized Pillow as an "ass" and a "consummate fool"; William Tecumseh Sherman saw him as a "mass of vanity, conceit, ignorance, ambition and want of truth." Quitman, according to another regular, was a "weak, vain, ignorant, ambitious" man who had earned the "supreme contempt" of nearly all the officers under his command. The volunteer officers retaliated in this verbal warfare by expressing the utmost contempt for the trim, polished, efficient West Pointers. Particularly galling to them was the custom of assigning regular troops to front line positions. This practice seemed to the volunteers to be unnecessarily discriminatory. On one occasion, it caused General Quitman to lodge a protest with General Scott in language so strong that the commanding general was forced to reprimand him for unmilitary conduct. Scott consistently defended his actions on the grounds that it was the commander's duty to put his strongest divisions forward.

Conflicts among officers were, however, mild in comparison with those among enlisted men. There is no avoiding the fact that these troubles were mainly the result of the attitudes and conduct of the men whom Taylor himself described as "the wild volunteers." Nowhere was the difference between the two groups more clearly discernible than in camp. The regulars, well aware of the importance to morale of their own health and comfort, carefully observed sanitation regulations, took good care of their arms and uniforms, and meticulously observed the daily routine. The volunteers, on the other hand, ignorant of even the rudiments of camp life, paid little or no attention to what they considered unimportant details. They frequently lived in filth and squalor, neglected or lost their arms and accouterments, and whenever possible ignored routine. They complained endlessly about the quarters provided them, about the meaningless routine of camp life, about the infrequency of payday, about army drill and discipline, and especially about the hated police duties such as chopping chaparral and clearing campsights. This combination of wilfulness and indifference was the cause of much sickness and suffering. Diarrhea, dysentery, and a variety of fevers played a large part in keeping the mortality rate higher in camp than on the field of battle.

From Washington to Mexico City, the volunteer soldiers in the Mexican War left a dismal trail of excesses and disorders. While they were still in the United States, there were incidents of abusing civilians, insulting women, and brawling among themselves. In the camp at Corpus Christi, theft was almost as popular a pursuit as gambling, and the existing disorder in the camp was increased by the easy accessibility of rotgut whiskey. "Almost all the houses in Corpus Christi," wrote one disgruntled officer, "are drinking houses put up since our arrival."

When the army moved into northern Mexico, the situation became even more serious. Desertions mounted at an increasing rate, and serious crimes such as rape and murder were not unknown. In Matamoros drunken officers and men committed numerous outrages on the inhabitants, and while en route to Camargo depredations of all sorts were reported. During the layover in that city, two volunteer officers actually fought a duel (this one lacked the color of the knife-fight in El Paso between two drunken officers of Doniphan's command). When Monterrey was finally taken, the pillage that had marked the route followed by the army was now visited almost exclusively on that city. "Nine tenths of the Americans here," complained one observer, "think it is a meritorious act to kill or rob a Mexican." The already bad situation there was made worse by the presence of tough, undisciplined Texas Rangers who engaged in what one eyewitness described as a "running warfare, embittered by old Texan feuds and waged between the half savage guerrillas of Mexico and the lynch gangs of the border." The situation in Monterrey deteriorated so that General Taylor finally had to muster the Texans out of service and send them home. Apprising the officials in Washington of this decision, he expressed the hope that order might now be restored in that area.

General Scott, in the Mexico City campaign, generally kept a tighter rein on his troops than had Taylor in northern Mexico.

But in spite of all his efforts, serious problems arose because of the conduct of the volunteers. At Veracruz, the guardhouses were kept well-stocked with frolicsome soldiers who had found the delights of the city irresistible. Much the same situation existed in Jalapa and Puebla. His greatest problems arose in Mexico City, where the occupation troops indulged themselves in an orgy of drinking, gambling, and brawling. Scott, because of the presence of the unruly Texans in his command, was faced with precisely the same problem that had dogged Taylor at Monterrey. He, too, was eventually forced to move them out of the city as a step toward restoration of order.

From time to time during the war, efforts were made to curb the excesses perpetrated by the volunteers. In some areas saloons were closed and in others the sale of alcohol to the troops was restricted and regulated. Punishments were meted out with increasing frequency, ranging from lashes laid on the bare back to hanging. Capital punishment was resorted to only in extreme cases, most often as the penalty for desertion. The volunteers considered the punishment for their misdeeds excessively severe. "More persons," wrote one of them indignantly, "have been shot or hung for various crimes by the American officers in Mexico during the past two years than would be capitally executed in the whole United States in the ordinary course of justice during ten years."

Difficulties with the citizen-soldier were by no means peculiar to the Mexican War; rather they were the general and inevitable result of a policy that had sent high-spirited, hastily enlisted, badly officered American troops, ignorant of even the most elementary rules of warfare, to invade a foreign country. Whatever else one might say about the volunteers, their enthusiasm was boundless. They were eager to win the war, but they wanted to win it on their own terms. Most of their misfortunes stemmed from their own vast ignorance of all things military, from their unconcealed contempt for those who did know something about the profession of arms, and from an inordinate fondness for spending time in what one soldier called the "Hells of Montezuma."

Whenever a nation goes to war, winning the war becomes the first order of business. In order to bring the combined resources of the country to bear against the enemy and to wage the war as effectively as possible with the means at hand, there should, ideally, be harmony between high-ranking military officers, co-operation between land and naval forces, and unity of purpose between the professional soldier and the citizen-soldier serving temporarily on active duty. In the war with Mexico, the United States enjoyed none of these advantages; in fact, we fought two quite different wars at the same time, one against the Mexicans and the other within the American military establishment. Our hidden war was gross and unedifying, marked by an unseemly scramble for preference among high-ranking officers, by jealous quarrels between the army and the navy, and by a continuing hostility between regulars and volunteers. Long after the rifles were stacked and the peace treaty signed, the effects of this inter-service squabbling were felt within the armed forces. No one has better summed up the whole messy situation than did young George Gordon Meade, who, in a moment of truth, wrote these words that might appropriately have been chiseled on marble in the nation's capital: "Well may we be grateful that we are at war with Mexico! Were it any other power, our gross follies would have been punished severely."

VII

The Diplomacy of War

From the moment that President Tyler, on March 1, 1845, in the closing hours of his tenure of office, signed the resolution providing for the annexation of Texas, the already strained relations between the United States and Mexico deteriorated. Within the week, the Mexican minister lodged a vigorous protest and abruptly left the country. The precarious position of the American minister to Mexico, growing worse now by the hour, soon became untenable, and with his return home all diplomatic intercourse between the two republics ceased, leaving unsolved a number of pressing grievances.

In addition to the explosive question of annexation, three other abrasive issues threatened Mexican-American amity. Still unsettled was the nagging question of claims against the Mexican government by American citizens. Over two million dollars in damages had been awarded to these claimants, but the Mexican government, more out of inability than unwillingness, had not yet made a payment. There was also the continuing dispute over the boundary of Texas. The Texans claimed everything south to the Rio Grande River, but the Mexicans were equally insistent that the boundary was the Nueces River; left in dispute was a strip of land some 150 miles wide. To complicate matters even more, the question of the future of California remained very much up in the air. Its extremely loose ties with Mexico suggested that the mother country's hold was at best a tenuous one. The swelling tide of migrants from the United States plainly indicated that California was on the way to becoming another Texas. Certainly American interest in California had been made obvious in the attempts of two presidents to purchase it, in the navy's premature seizure of Monterey in 1842, and in the agile maneuverings of the United States Consul Thomas O. Larkin, whose activities both alarmed and annoyed Mexican authorities.

These were the outstanding difficulties with Mexico that President Polk inherited in his new office. Since they were all to some degree involved in the question of peace or war, his attitude toward them was bound to be of considerable significance. On the question of claims, the President was somewhat vague, for, while he felt that the claims awarded to American citizens should definitely be paid, he also intimated a willingness for the United States government to assume the obligation as part of what he hoped would be a sizable real estate transaction between the two nations. On the other two points, however, his position was unequivocal. Insofar as the Texas boundary was concerned, Polk felt that annexation carried with it the obligation to defend the area claimed by Texans as their own, and he therefore insisted upon the Rio Grande line. As for California, he considered its acquisition one of the primary objectives of his administration, and he so confided to one of his cabinet members on his first day in office.

The Mexican War

Clearly, then, the aims and objectives of Mexican and American foreign policy were in direct conflict. In an attempt to avoid the impending clash, Polk made one last effort to settle differences through negotiation by sending John Slidell to Mexico with authority to discuss all three major problems. With the refusal of the Mexican government even to receive Slidell, all hope for a diplomatic settlement vanished; on January 13, 1846, immediately after receiving news of the rejection of the Slidell mission, the President ordered General Taylor to move his army from Corpus Christi to the Rio Grande, an order that altered the situation by making war a probability rather than a mere possibility. Polk would undoubtedly have preferred to achieve a satisfactory settlement by diplomacy, but when diplomacy failed he showed surprising readiness to resort to war. This readiness he defended on the grounds of his obligation to the Texans, his determination to secure California, and the refusal of the Mexicans to negotiate.

War was not long in coming. As so often happens when hostile nations continue to annoy each other, an "incident" eventually occurred and the official declaration of war became a mere formality. But even as the war was being vigorously prosecuted, the door was kept open for the possible resumption of negotiations. In his war message of May 11, the President was careful to point out that his country was ready to negotiate whenever the Mexicans should indicate a willingness even to listen to our proposals. On the following day the State Department issued instructions to our diplomats abroad setting forth the official position of the administration. These instructions not only expressed regrets that the situation had become intolerable; they also reiterated a willingness to restore friendly relations through a diplomatic settlement. The war with Mexico, according to this official statement, was being fought "solely for the purpose of conquering an honourable and permanent peace." A further reflection of the government's desire for peaceful settlement was contained in the instructions forwarded to General Taylor, at that time fighting in northern Mexico, which expressly directed him to use any opportunity to open negotiations with the enemy.

The President's overtures were somewhat misleading, for the only settlement Polk was interested in was one wholly on his own terms. Nowhere is this more clearly apparent than in his dealings with the English, whose sympathy for Mexico and distrust of the United States were sufficiently strong to make plausible the rumor of their possible intervention. Early in the war, Lord Aberdeen tendered an offer of mediation which, in spite of the State Department's studied indifference, was repeated by his successor, Lord Palmerston. In the final analysis, however, it was military success rather than astute diplomacy that prevented foreign intervention; Taylor's unbroken string of victories in northern Mexico not only made intervention unlikely, but also made mediation seemingly unnecessary, a fact that was finally relayed officially to England with obvious relish.

Toward Mexico, nevertheless, the government continued to extend the olive branch. On July 27, after having defeated the Mexicans at Palo Alto and the Resaca de la Palma, with Matamoros occupied by American troops and Taylor's army en route to Monterrey, Secretary of State James Buchanan again forwarded to his Mexican counterpart an invitation to resume negotiations, but his efforts were wasted. Contrary to official expectations, American military successes in the north did little more than cause a sober reappraisal by the Mexicans. Not even the capture of the important city of Monterrey brought them to the point of seeking a negotiated peace. Far removed from the scenes of actual combat and comforted by the fact that American victories in northern Mexico could never prove decisive, the government in Mexico City sustained itself with the futile hope that the invading army might yet be defeated. Negotiation with the enemy continued to be unthinkable. This intransigence unwittingly placed the United States government in a difficult position. Unable either to conquer Mexico under existing military plans or even to open negotiations with her for peace, the administration in Washington was brought face to face with the threat of stalemate on both the military and diplomatic fronts.

It was this very threat of stalemate that brought about a sudden reversal of policy by the United States government. Convinced at long last of the futility of attempting to knock Mexico out of the war by winning military victories on the northern periphery, Polk abandoned his original plan and threw the full weight of his support behind the proposed Veracruz expedition. This new operation was specifically designed to "conquer a peace" by carrying the war to the very heart of Mexico. In order to facilitate a treaty, the President decided to send a diplomatic representative with Scott's army.

For this crucial mission, Polk selected Nicholas Trist, Chief Clerk of the State Department, who soon thereafter left the capital and headed for the front, armed with three important documents. The first of these was a letter dated April 15, 1847, from Secretary Buchanan to the Mexican Minister of Foreign Relations, stating that the United States government would make no further attempt to renew negotiations until the Mexicans showed some willingness to do so but calling that official's attention to the fact that an American commissioner, fully authorized to negotiate with any properly delegated Mexican representative, had been attached to American army headquarters. Secretary Buchanan, apparently more concerned with effect than with accuracy, identified Commissioner Trist to the Mexican government as "the officer second in rank in the American department of foreign affairs" and as a person who possessed "the entire confidence" of President Polk. This was, to say the least, a gross overstatement, in view of subsequent developments. The second document in Trist's portfolio was a draft of a proposed treaty. While this draft contained fairly specific American demands, still it allowed to the commissioner some discretion over boundary lines and the amount of money to be paid Mexico. The third paper in his possession was an order from the Secretary of the Treasury authorizing him to draw upon the government up to three million dollars from a fund that had been reluctantly appropriated by the Congress in March at the President's insistence, to cover what was described with deliberate ambiguity as "extraordinary expenses." It was an open secret that the money was to be used to facilitate negotiations.

After Trist's arrival in Mexico, diplomatic activities were temporarily shelved while he and General Scott indulged in their quarrel. Trist's independent attitude fully aroused Scott's anger. The General was already annoyed at the government's unsettling instructions making it clear that it would be his duty to suspend military operations on the recommendation of a State Department functionary. The violent exchange of correspondence between Scott and Trist not only insured their complete alienation, it also delayed for a time any possibility of opening other negotions with the enemy. In fact, it was not until the army reached Puebla that the differences between the two men were finally settled. Following this reconciliation, however, they became fast friends and for the remainder of the war worked well together toward their common objective.

Having successfully negotiated a peace with General Scott, Trist now attempted to do as well with the Mexicans. In June, 1847, while still at Puebla, Trist wrote to the resident English minister asking him to serve as an intermediary between the two warring governments. In response to this request, a representative from the English embassy hastened to Puebla, picked up the letter from Secretary of State Buchanan and departed with it for Mexico City. In the capital, however, no one seemed to know exactly what to do with the communication. The foreign office passed it along to Santa Anna, who hastily forwarded it to the Congress, who, in turn, referred it back to El Presidente. The reason for this juggling act was a law, passed earlier in the year by the Mexican Congress, designating anyone a "traitor" who even dared to listen to terms offered by the United States. Behind the scenes, however, the wily Santa Anna, sensing the possibilities in the situation, determined to gain whatever advantage he could. He opened secret negotiations with Trist. Approximately two weeks after his message had been sent to Mexico City, Trist was approached through intermediaries who informed him that Santa Anna might possibly be induced to begin negotiations under certain conditions. According to these messengers, the conditions were, first, that Santa Anna be given an immediate payment of ten thousand dollars; second, that the American army move out of Puebla and make a demonstration against Mexico City thereby helping create an atmosphere more conducive to open-

General Santa Anna

Rackensackers on the Rampage

ing negotiations; and finally, that Santa Anna be paid one million dollars after a treaty was successfully concluded.

The bait was extremely tempting to both Trist and Scott, who, confident of the desires of both major political parties in the United States for peace and spurred on by visions of the honor and prestige that would in all likelihood accrue to the responsible agents, proved only too eager to swallow it. There were two serious obstacles, however; one was a natural reluctance to incur the stigma that might attach to any treaty secured through bribery. The other was where to find the ten thousand dollars even if his reluctance could be overcome. Needless to say, both obstacles were quickly removed. Scott called a meeting of his officers and discussed frankly with them the legitimacy of buying a treaty. Some members of the staff opposed the proposal on the grounds that a bribe was wrong in principle, that it was inconsistent with American theory and practice, and that it would embarrass the nation. General Quitman, in particular, denounced the scheme as one that would inevitably prove humiliating to the American people. Scott personally defended the proposal by claiming that it affected the integrity of no one. "The overture," he pointed out, "if corrupt, came from parties already corrupted." Then, arguing that Santa Anna had voluntarily placed himself on the auction block, the General announced his decision to take advantage of the existing opportunity. Persuaded that a precedent had been established by our dealings with various Indian tribes as well as the Barbary pirates and convinced that the cost would in the long run prove cheaper than a conquest of the Mexican capital, Scott freely assumed all responsibility for his decision. In short, the General arrived at the comfortable conclusion that peace (the end) justified bribery (the means).

The Mexican War

Having reached this decision, the next problem was where to find the money with which to implement it. Congress had deliberately attached a number of strings to the three million dollar appropriation, the most important of which was that it could be spent only in the event that a treaty had been negotiated. Since there was no legal way this money could be used to pay the ten thousand dollar down payment, General Scott came to the rescue by supplying the needed amount from his secret service fund. As it happened, the payment made to Santa Anna turned out to be nothing more than a donation. The pressure of Mexican public opinion effectively prevented Santa Anna's even making a suggestion that negotiations be resumed. The net result of this clumsy attempt to secure a treaty was the loss of ten thousand dollars and a strengthening of the Mexican position by allowing the troops in Mexico City additional time to work on defenses.

Undaunted by failure, Trist continued to travel with the army hoping that another and more rewarding opportunity for a peaceful settlement might present itself. His patience was finally rewarded as American troops were smashing their way nearer to the gates of the city. After the defeat at Churubusco on August 20, Santa Anna, hoping not only to keep the Americans out of the city but also to gain desperately needed time in which to reorganize his shattered army, once again turned to his favorite pastime, playing cat-and-mouse with his adversaries. That night after the battle, an envoy arrived at Scott's headquarters seeking a suspension of hostilities as a prelude to the opening of negotiations and since the moment seemed propitious for securing a treaty, Scott was easily persuaded to hold his position and not attempt to force an entry into the city. Both he and Trist, in their eagerness to obtain a negotiated

peace, were easily convinced that a forward movement of the
army might cause a general dispersal of officials from the capital, leaving no one with whom to negotiate. To forestall this
eventuality, Scott, on the morning of August 21, wrote a conciliatory note to Santa Anna reminding him that a peace commissioner was still available and offering to grant a short armistice in order to facilitate negotiations. In a reply carefully
worded to make it appear that the United States was seeking
a cessation of hostilities, Santa Anna agreed with Scott and
named several Mexican officers who would meet with the
Americans to discuss the details of an armistice. After two days
of incessant wrangling, terms were agreed upon and after
they were ratified by both commanders the way was cleared
for the diplomats to get down to work.

The first meeting was scheduled for August 27, but a delay
was threatened because of the difficulties experienced by Santa
Anna in finding responsible persons who would agree to serve
on the commission. Few were willing to incur the ill will that
any fruitful negotiations would almost certainly create. Santa
Anna, himself, felt constrained to justify his actions publicly
by issuing a proclamation making it clear that Scott had asked
for the armistice. He further soothed the fears and suspicions
of his people by reassuring them that there was no danger of
his yielding peacefully to the Americans when their troops
and cannon had not inspired him with fear.

From the very beginning of the discussions, there was little
hope of success. The United States demanded that Mexico
recognize the Rio Grande boundary and cede both California
and New Mexico in exchange for a stipulated sum of money.
The Mexicans, on the other hand, were willing to give up their
claim to Texas and to cede upper California to the United

States, but they flatly refused to give up title to New Mexico and insisted that a buffer state, under international guaranty, be created out of the disputed area between the Nueces and the Rio Grande. Additional Mexican demands for indemnification, the exclusion of slavery from any territory acquired from Mexico, and a return of the San Patricio deserters captured at Churubusco made reconciliation clearly impossible. On September 2, the sessions ended. Three days later the Mexican foreign office declared American terms to be unacceptable and submitted a counterproposal that was immediately rejected. Upon this collapse of negotiations, hostilities were once again resumed. Scott and Trist had been given a second lesson in the gentle art of diplomacy by Santa Anna. From that time on both men were firmly convinced that if there was to be any peace at all, it would have to be a conquered one.

Fortunately for the Polk administration, American arms were more successful than American diplomacy. On September 14, 1847, the army marched into Mexico City. Not even the occupation of their capital brought the Mexicans to the bargaining table, however. Their reluctance to come to terms with the enemy was rooted in a number of causes: a Mexican pride that made it exceedingly difficult to face up to defeat, a general political instability in which decision-making was effectively frustrated, a desire on the part of many inside Mexico to break the army's hold on the state, a widespread suspicion that the small, dissension-ridden army of occupation would prove unequal to its task, and, finally, a not altogether groundless hope that political quarrels within the United States might help secure more favorable terms. With these varied and disruptive influences working against peace, there seemed little likelihood of an immediate settlement. The American army dug in for what promised to be an extended occupation.

In the United States, meanwhile, pressure on the administration to bring the war to an end steadily increased. The frequently expressed criticisms of our inept diplomacy and the increasingly devastating attacks by Whig opponents of the administration forced Polk to harden his attitude toward Mexico. Assuming the lofty position that the defeated enemy must sue for peace in Washington, the President had Trist recalled on October 6. Six weeks elapsed before the message actually reached Trist, however, and in the intervening period significant developments had occurred which profoundly altered the situation in Mexico. The election of Pedro Anaya as interim president of Mexico signified an increased interest in terminating the conflict. But just as Trist was preparing to capitalize on this break, the letter of recall was delivered to him. The crestfallen diplomat was preparing for his return home when word arrived from the Mexican foreign office that commissioners had been named to enter into negotiations for peace. Receipt of this intelligence placed him in a quandary; should he return home as ordered or should he deliberately disobey the orders of his superior and take advantage of the opportunity to draw up a treaty? After long deliberation, Trist, certain that the Mexican government desired a treaty and that a refusal to negotiate would prove disastrous to the peace party in Mexico and convinced that the administration in Washington did not understand the current situation, decided to remain in Mexico and negotiate a treaty. On December 4, the day he was scheduled to leave the country, he wrote these words home to his wife: "Knowing it to be the very last chance and impressed with the dreadful consequences to our country which cannot fail to attend the loss of that chance, I decided today at noon to attempt to make a treaty; the decision is altogether my own. . . ." Though technically an unemployed diplomat, Trist unabashedly opened negotiations with the Mexican government—but not until after he had written a sixty-odd-page letter of justification to President Polk. The length of this letter did nothing to lessen Polk's indignation at the presumptuousness of the man he now denounced as an "impudent and unqualified scoundrel."

Throughout early January, 1848, Trist, anxious to complete his work before more positive orders arrived from Washington barring him from acting on behalf of the government, met daily with the Mexican commissioners in an all-out effort to hammer out an agreement. Arguments dragged on over boundary guaranties, over the removal of United States troops, and over the amount of money to be paid to Mexico. With time running out, Trist, in desperation, resorted to a bluff by abruptly declaring on January 29, an end to the negotiations. The Mexican government, threatened by revolt from within and conquest from without, yielded to the inevitable.

On February 2, 1848, the Treaty of Guadalupe Hidalgo, designed to end the "calamities" of war, to re-establish peace and friendship between the United States and Mexico and to assure "concord, harmony and mutual confidence" in the future, was signed. Most of the twenty-three articles contained in the treaty dealt with such miscellaneous topics as the cessation of hostilities, the evacuation of Mexican territory and the return of public property, the rights of Mexican nationals, commercial relations, rights of navigation, future arbitration policies, and ratification procedures. But the heart of the treaty was compressed into a few short articles; these ceded California and New Mexico to the United States and confirmed the American claim to Texas along the Rio Grande line in exchange for a payment of fifteen million dollars and the assumption by the United States government of claims against Mexico by American citizens amounting to an additional three and a quarter million dollars.

A copy of the treaty was sent with all possible speed to Washington and its arrival in the capital on February 19 placed Polk in the unenviable position of having to decide whether or not to repudiate the highly satisfactory handiwork of his discredited subordinate. Good sense ultimately prevailed and the President, yielding to the combined power of logic and political pressure, forwarded it to the Senate on Washington's birthday. On the tenth of March, with only minor adjustments, the Senate ratified the treaty by a vote of 38 to 14.

In Mexico, meanwhile, the treaty had encountered unexpectedly powerful opposition. Any terms acquiescing in the alienation of territory were *ipso facto* repugnant to a large segment of the Mexican population and when its contents were made public on February 6, bitter denunciations of the government were voiced. Faced with what appeared to be a mounting crisis, the executive neatly sidestepped the issue by handing over the treaty to the Mexican Congress, thereby shifting to the "people's representatives" the onus for making what was bound to be an unpopular decision. After a hectic debate, the "people's representatives" bowed to the inevitable and voted to accept the treaty.

On the thirtieth of May, 1848, ratifications were duly exchanged by the two governments and preparations were immediately begun for the evacuation of American troops stationed in Mexico. On the twelfth of June, following a brief ceremony, the occupation troops marched briskly out of Mexico City, and by the end of July the last detachment of American soldiers had boarded their transports in the harbor at Veracruz.

The war with Mexico was over.

Important Dates

1845   Tyler signs resolution to annex Texas, March 1
Polk inaugurated, March 4
Taylor moves to Corpus Christi, July 25
Slidell mission sent to Mexico, November
Texas formally admitted into the Union, December 29

1846   Taylor ordered to the Rio Grande, January 13
Slidell mission fails, March 21
Taylor arrives on the Rio Grande, March 28
Mexican troops attack Thornton's command, April 25
Battle of Palo Alto, May 8
Battle of Resaca de la Palma; Frémont returns to California
   from Oregon, May 9
Polk sends war message to Congress, May 11
War declared by United States government, May 13
Taylor occupies Matamoros, May 17–18
Kearny begins march to New Mexico, June 5
"Bear Flag Republic" proclaimed, July 4
Sloat seizes Monterey (Calif.), July 7
Taylor occupies Camargo, July 14
Stockton occupies Los Angeles, August 12
Santa Anna returns from exile, August 16

The Mexican War

Kearny occupies Santa Fe, August 18
Battle of Monterrey, September 20–24
Californians revolt at Los Angeles, September 22–23
Wool departs for Chihuahua; Kearny leaves New Mexico for California, September 25
Wool occupies Monclova, October 29
Conner occupies Tampico, November 14
Taylor occupies Saltillo, November 16
Scott appointed to command the Veracruz expedition, November 18
Wool occupies Parras, December 5
Battle of San Pascual, December 6
Doniphan expedition leaves Valverde; Kearny reaches San Diego, December 12
Doniphan's fight at El Brazito, December 25
Doniphan occupies El Paso, December 27

1847   Scott withdraws troops from Taylor, January 3
Californians defeated at the Battle of San Gabriel, January 8
Stockton reoccupies Los Angeles, January 10
Taylor advances to Agua Nueva, February 5
Taylor takes up position at Buena Vista, February 21
Battle of Buena Vista, February 22–23
Doniphan fights Battle of Sacramento, February 28
Doniphan occupies Chihuahua, March 1
Amphibious landing below Veracruz, March 9
Surrender of Veracruz, March 29
Scott begins advance inland from Veracruz, April 8
Nicholas Trist appointed peace commissioner, April 15
Battle of Cerro Gordo, April 18
Worth occupies Perote, April 22
Worth occupies Puebla, May 15
Battle of Contreras, August 19
Battle of Churubusco, August 20
Armistice proclaimed at Tacubaya, August 24
Armistice terminated, September 6
Battle of Molino del Rey, September 8
Battle of Chapultepec, September 13
Scott occupies Mexico City, September 14

Important Dates

Santa Anna relinquishes the presidency, September 16
Polk orders recall of Trist, October 6
Trist receives order of recall, November 16
Trist decides to remain in Mexico, December 4

1848   Scott relieved of command by Polk, January 13
Treaty of Guadelupe Hidalgo signed, February 2
Treaty ratified by United States Senate, March 10
Treaty ratified by Mexican government, March 25
Ratifications normally exchanged, May 30
American troops evacuate Mexico City, June 12

Suggested Reading

By far the best general account of the war is Justin H. Smith's two-volume *The War with Mexico* (1919), though there are a number of good one-volume works such as Alfred H. Bill, *Rehearsal for Conflict* (1947), Bernard De Voto, *Year of Decision, 1846* (1943), Robert S. Henry, *Story of the Mexican War* (1950), and Nathaniel W. Stephenson, *Texas and the Mexican War* (1921). Volume VII of John B. McMaster's multivolume *History of the People of the United States* (1910), Volume II of George L. Rives's *The United States and Mexico, 1821–48* (1913), and Cadmus M. Wilcox' *History of the Mexican War* (1892) also provide detailed accounts. For histories written during or immediately after the war, see Nathan C. Brooks, *A Complete History of the Mexican War* (1849), William S. Henry, *Campaign Sketches of the War with Mexico* (1847), William Jay, *A Review of the Causes and the Consequences of the Mexican War* (1849), John S. Jenkins, *History of the War between the United States and Mexico* (1849), and R. S. Ripley, *The War with Mexico* (1849). The unpublished manuscript "History of the Mexican War," written by George Wilkins Kendall and now gathering dust in the archives of the University of Texas, is an excellent firsthand account by the man who covered the war as a reporter for the New Orleans *Picayune*.

Biographies of figures prominent in the Mexican War are not

Suggested Reading

plentiful. For the ablest works on the two best-known military figures of the war see Charles W. Elliott, *Winfield Scott, the Soldier and the Man* (1937), and Holman Hamilton, *Zachary Taylor, Soldier of the Republic* (1941). Other readable lives of these two soldiers include A. D. Howden Smith, *Old Fuss and Feathers* (1937), Brainerd Dyer, *Zachary Taylor* (1946), and Silas Bent McKinley and Silas Bent, *Old Rough and Ready* (1946). For biographies of other military figures see Allan Nevins, *Frémont, Pathmarker of the West* (1955), Edward S. Wallace, *General William Jenkins Worth* (1953), Samuel J. Bayard, *Sketch of the Life of Commodore Robert F. Stockton* (1856), and J. F. H. Claiborne, *Life and Correspondence of John A. Quitman* (1860). Douglas S. Freeman's monumental biography of Lee (1934), T. Harry Williams' study of Beauregard (1955) and Hudson Strode's life of Jefferson Davis (1955) also contain interesting chapters on the Mexican War phase of these men's careers. Eugene I. McCormac's life of Polk (1922) will continue to be the best available biography of the wartime President until the second volume of Charles G. Sellers' work is published. William N. Chambers, *Old Bullion Benton, Senator from the New West* (1956) is a recent work on one of Washington's most influential politicians during the war. Wilfred H. Callcott's life of Santa Anna (1936) is the best biography in English of the Mexican leader.

Among the most interesting of the memoirs, diaries, and other accounts of participants in the war are Robert Anderson, *An Artillery Officer in the Mexican War* (1911), E. J. Blackwood (ed.), *To Mexico with Scott: Letters of Captain E. Kirby Smith to His Wife* (1917), Samuel E. Chamberlain, *My Confession* (1956), the *Memoirs* of Scott (1864) and Frémont (1887) and the letters of Taylor (1908), George C. Furber, *The Twelve Months Volunteer* (1849), Ethan Allen Hitchcock, *Fifty Years in Camp and Field* (1909), John R. Kenly, *Memoirs of a Maryland Volunteer* (1873), George Meade, *The Life and Letters of George Gordon Meade* (1913), William S. Myers (ed.), *The Mexican War Diary of George B. McClellan* (1917), Allan Nevins (ed.), *Polk: The Diary of a President, 1845–1849* (1929), J. Jacob Oswandel, *Notes of the Mexican War, 1846–47–48* (1885), Milo M. Quaife (ed.), *The Diary of James K. Polk during His Presidency, 1845 to 1849* (1910), and T. Harry Williams (ed.), *With Beauregard in Mexico: The Mexican War Reminiscences of P. G. T. Beauregard* (1956).

The Mexican War

For the navy's role in the Mexican War see P. S. P. Conner, *The Home Squadron* (1896), Raphael Semmes, *Service Afloat and Ashore in the Mexican War* (1851), and Fitch W. Taylor, *The Broad Pennant* (1848).

Official government records pertaining to the war are included in various documents of the Twenty-ninth and Thirtieth Congresses. For specific references to the war, see the following: Twenty-ninth Congress, first session (*House Executive Documents* 197, 207, 209; *House Document* 196; *Senate Documents* 337, 378, 388, 392); Twenty-ninth Congress, second session (*House Executive Document* 119; *House Document* 88; *Senate Executive Documentment* 1; *Senate Document* 107); Thirtieth Congress, first session (*House Executive Documents* 17, 40, 59, 60, 62; *House Document* 56; *Senate Executive Documents* 1, 14, 36, 65).

Other works of particular interest include Fayette Copeland, *Kendall of the Picayune* (1943), Philip St. George Cooke, *The Conquest of New Mexico and California* (1878), John T. Hughes, *Doniphan's Expedition* (1848), Francis Baylies, *Major General Wool's Campaign in Mexico* (1851), J. S. Reeves, *American Diplomacy under Tyler and Polk* (1907), and Walter P. Webb, *The Texas Rangers* (1935). To see the war through Mexican eyes consult Walter V. Scholes's ably edited version of José Fernando Ramíriz, *Mexico during the War with the United States* (1950), and Albert Ramsey's translation of Ramón Alcaraz, *The Other Side; or Notes for the History of the War between Mexico and the United States* (1850).

John Frost's *Pictorial History of Mexico and the Mexican War* (1848) contains a wealth of illustrated material, and the color plates in George Wilkins Kendall's *The War between the United States and Mexico, Illustrated* (1851) are magnificent. Chamberlain's water colors, now located at the San Jacinto Museum of History in Houston, are delightful, as are those in William H. Meyers, *Naval Sketches of the War in California* (1939). For other illustrations, see appropriate sections of *An Album of American Battle Art* (1947) and Roy Meredith's *The American Wars* (1955).

Acknowledgments

I am indebted to Alfred A. Knopf, Inc., for permission to use the map of the United States and Mexico, 1846–48, originally published in Alfred Hoyt Bill's *Rehearsal for Conflict* (copyright 1947 by Alfred H. Bill) and to the San Jacinto Museum of History for permission to reproduce illustrations in their possession.

I would also like to express my appreciation to Mrs. Elizabeth O'Bryan and Miss Kay Voetmann for typing and retyping the manuscript.

Index

Index

Corpus Christi, Texas, 10, 11, 132; camp life at, 145
Coyoacán: Scott concentrates army at, 90

Devil's Fort, 36
Doniphan, Alexander W.: leads expedition against Chihuahua, 59–62
"Doniphan's Thousand." *See* Doniphan, Alexander W.
Durango, 44

El Brazito, 60
Ellis, Powhatan: chargé d'affaires to Mexico, 18
El Paso, 145; surrenders to Doniphan, 61
El Peñon: fortifications on, 86
El Soldado (fort), 36; falls to Worth, 38
Encero: Santa Anna headquarters, 77
England, 9; sympathy for Mexico, 151; minister acts as intermediary, 154
European intervention: possibility of, 21, 22, 151
European military system: as employed in New World, 4

Fannin, James, 15
Federation Hill: fortification of, 35, 36; captured by Worth, 38
Fort Brown, 31; construction of, 12; shelling of, 29, 32
Fort Leavenworth, 57
Fort Marcy, 59
Fort Polk: construction of, 12;

defenses improved, 28. *See also* Point Isabel
France, 9
Frémont, John C., 63, 66, 67; and "Bear Flag Revolt," 64; in command of California Battalion, 65; negotiates Treaty of Cahuenga, 69; conflict with Kearny, 140, 141; relationship with Stockton, 140, 141; court-martial of, 141; resigns from army, 142
Frémont expedition, 63, 64

Gaines, Edmund P.: Taylor's letter to, 112
General Order 20, 5
Goliad, Texas: massacre at, 15, 16
Gorostiza, Manuel, 19
Grant, Ulysses S., 5
Guadalupe Hidalgo, 85, 86, 98; Treaty of, 6, 160, 161
Guerrero: overthrows Victoria, 17
Guerrilla warfare: in Mexico City, 99; on American wagon trains, 100
Gulf of Mexico: Mexican ports in, 25

Harney, William S., 121, 122, 134
Havana, Cuba: Santa Anna in, 26
Herrera, José: overthrow of, 10; administration of, 18
Hidalgo Revolt of 1810, 17
Hooker, Joe, 6

173

Index

THE CHICAGO HISTORY OF AMERICAN CIVILIZATION

DANIEL J. BOORSTIN, EDITOR

Edmund S. Morgan, *The Birth of the Republic: 1763–89*

Marcus Cunliffe, *The Nation Takes Shape: 1789–1837*

John Hope Franklin, *Reconstruction: After the Civil War*

Samuel P. Hays, *The Response to Industrialism: 1885–1914*

William E. Leuchtenburg, *The Perils of Prosperity: 1914–32*

Dexter Perkins, *The New Age of Franklin Roosevelt: 1932–45*

Herbert Agar, *The Price of Power: America since 1945*

*   *   *

Robert H. Bremner, *American Philanthropy*

*Harry L. Coles, *The War of 1812*

Richard M. Dorson, *American Folklore*

John Tracy Ellis, *American Catholicism*

Nathan Glazer, *American Judaism*

William T. Hagan, *American Indians*

Winthrop S. Hudson, *American Protestantism*

Maldwyn Allen Jones, *American Immigration*

Robert G. McCloskey, *The American Supreme Court*

Howard H. Peckham, *The War for Independence: A Military History*

Howard H. Peckham, *The Colonial Wars: 1689–1762*

Henry Pelling, *American Labor*

Charles P. Roland, *The Confederacy*

Otis A. Singletary, *The Mexican War*

John F. Stover, *American Railroads*

*Bernard A. Weisberger, *The American Newspaperman*

* Available in cloth only. All other books published in both cloth and paperback editions.